Getting Paid: an architect's guide to fee recovery claims

Nicholas J. Carnell and Stephen Yakeley

RIBA Enterprises

© Nicholas J. Carnell, 2003

Published by RIBA Enterprises Ltd, 1–3 Dufferin Street, London EC1Y 8NA

ISBN 1 85946 072 0
Product Code 20331

The right of Nicholas J. Carnell to be identified as the Author of this Work has been asserted in accordance with the Copyright, Designs and Patents Act 1988.

All rights reserved. No part of this publication may be reproduced, stored in a retrieval system, or transmitted, in any form or by any means, electronic, mechanical, photocopying, recording or otherwise, without prior permission of the copyright owner.

British Library Cataloguing in Publications Data
A catalogue record for this book is available from the British Library

Authors: Nicholas J. Carnell and Stephen Yakeley
Publisher: Geoff Denner
Commissioning Editor: Matthew Thompson
Project Editor: Katy Banyard
Editor: Elizabeth Davison
Designed by: US²Design
Printed and bound by Bell & Bain

While every effort has been made to check the accuracy of the information given in this book, readers should always make their own checks. Neither the Author nor the Publisher accept any responsibility for mis-statements made in it or misunderstandings arising from it.

Contents

Introduction   1

1 An intractable problem   5
An artist or an administrator?   5
In the firing line   5
The uneven playing field   7
Administrative factors   7
Economic factors   8
Procedural factors   9

2 The indemnity trap   11

3 The right to payment   17
Housing Grants, Construction and Regeneration Act 1996   18
Uncertainty in the appointment   20
Uncertainties arising in the course of the works   22

4 Appointments   31
Contractual relations   31
Appointments with fear   33
The danger with shortcuts   39
Home-made forms of appointment   43
Collateral warranties   44

5 Set-off and counterclaims   49
Set-off and counterclaims distinguished   49
Restrictions imposed by statute   53
Restrictions imposed by contract   54

6 The decision to proceed   57
The end of the affair   57
What should be done?   61
    Is it worth attempting to confront the client and bring matters to a head?   61

Can work be suspended or cease altogether?	61
Should insurers be notified?	63
Once a threat of litigation is made, can it be withdrawn?	65
Choice of proceedings	65
Insolvency procedures	65
Adjudication	66
Mediation	67
Arbitration	68
Litigation	68

7 Litigation and arbitration — 71

Introduction	71
Litigation or arbitration: which to choose?	76
Overriding objectives and protocols	78
Litigation procedure	85
Starting proceedings	85
Particulars of claim	86
Acknowledgement of service and defence	87
Allocation	88
The small claims track	89
The fast track	89
The multi-track	91
Expert evidence	92
Summary judgement	93
Preliminary issues	95
Security for costs	95
Disclosure	97
Part 36 offers and payments into court	98
Service out of the jurisdiction	100
Arbitration procedure	101
Introduction	101
Fee recovery claims in arbitration	102
Costs	105

8 Adjudication 109
Introduction 109
The advantages 110
Some disadvantages 112
How adjudication works 113
A few examples 116
Applying this to architects' fee claims 117
Enforcement 120

9 Legal expenses insurance 123
Introduction 123
Pre-event cover 123
After the event cover 123
How it works 124
CFAs, success fees and premiums 125
Some pros and cons 128

Appendix 1: Case Study 1 materials 133
Appendix 2: Checklist 136
Appendix 3: Glossary of terms 137
Appendix 4: Claim form and particulars of claim 138
Appendix 5: Conditional fee agreement 142

Index 154

Abbreviations

AQ
allocation questionnaire

ATE
after the event insurance cover

CFA
conditional fee agreement

CMC
case management conference

CPR
Civil Procedure Rules (SI 1998/3132)

HGCRA 1996
Housing Grants, Construction and Regeneration Act 1996

PEC
pre-event insurance cover

TeCSA
Technology and Construction Court Solicitors Association

Authors' Note

Whilst most architects find great satisfaction from the sheer pleasure of designing buildings, architecture can be difficult, even a cruel profession. And there can be hardly anything more devastating than to have a client who owes a substantial sum who suddenly refuses to pay. The work on which the architect had devoted so much passion is claimed to be worthless. Worse, the anticipated fee had been factored into cash flow forecasts; the bank overdraft was negotiated on the back of it; next month's staff salary payments (not to mention partners' drawings) depend on it – and suddenly it has evaporated. It quickly dawns that the ways of enforcing the collection of the fee are expensive, risky and time consuming.

This book, boring though it may seem to anyone who has not faced the gut-wrenching fear that such a predicament engenders, should be read by architects in private practice before a problem arises. Much can be done by taking prudent measures to avoid such problems occurring or if they do, in substantially improving the chances of achieving an acceptable outcome.

For those unfortunate architects already facing such a problem (and almost all will do so several times in their careers), this book will help them analyse their predicament and plot the most suitable course.

Nicholas J. Carnell is a partner at Kennedys and specialises in construction law. He is also a qualified mediator, a Fellow of the Chartered Institute of Arbitrators and a highly regarded author.

Stephen Yakeley is a director of Yakeley Associates and has been a practising architect for forty years. He has served on a number of RIBA Committees, particularly the Committee that drafts the standard forms of appointment between architect and client.

Introduction

In his helpful *A Guide to Keeping Out of Trouble*,[1] Owen Luder offers the view that architecture is a challenging and exciting profession but one which must be conducted within the constraints of a modern business. To refine this view slightly, while many architects have the possibility granted to very few professionals – to leave their work as a lasting monument to their talent – the paradox is that architects frequently experience greater problems than other professionals in securing payment for their work.

Getting paid can be crucial to a practice. Architects often have fewer clients compared with other professional firms of similar size. Hence, one client can represent a large proportion of a firm's income at any given time. The consequences of non-payment by a particular client can present severe financial difficulties and can sometimes drive a firm into insolvency.

In many cases this arises out of the inequality of bargaining power between the architect and his or her client. In others it is a function of the way in which many architects conduct their practices, in which perhaps more stress is laid on the creative than the commercial. In both, the difficulties, expense and uncertainty of pursuing legal remedies, would seem to make fee claims too risky a business for all but the most determined.

Until recently, architects faced a 'triple whammy' when a client did not pay:

- first, the practice was weakened financially by the disturbance to its cash flow;
- second, if the practice decided to resort to law it had to fund its legal team as well as its own time in fighting the action (with the risk of being ordered to pay the other side's costs if it lost);
- third, there was the risk that a defendant client could ask the court to order that the architect should provide security for costs; in other words that the architect should either pay a sum of money into court or provide a bond or other security in respect of the other side's costs in case the architect lost and was ordered to pay the client's costs.

Getting Paid

It is small wonder that few architects took steps to collect fees which were not paid. Recent changes to the way legal actions are conducted, a new method of employing lawyers and revised standard architect/client contracts make these difficulties considerably easier to overcome. This book is meant to help architects understand and hopefully to overcome these formidable hurdles.

The approach adopted here is to start by describing the problems which may face an architects' practice in pursuing fee claims, then looking at the practical and contractual steps which might be taken to reduce these risks. The book then considers the remedies which exist and the steps which can be taken to maximise the prospects of success.

To use an old-fashioned term this book is intended to be a 'remembrancer' – a convenient guide which can be turned to for help in dealing with day to day problems. It contains very little discussion of legal theory. References to cases have been kept to a minimum and in the main are confined to endnotes and appendices. In planning the work, the authors took the view that it was likely to be more useful to discuss particular issues and to illustrate them by case studies and practical examples than by detailed consideration of precedents. There are good reasons for this. First, it may be said with some justification that the law reports only deal with projects which have gone wrong and where the parties have failed to find a way of resolving their differences. Second, the cases are often of limited assistance: in many instances they are concerned with unique factual scenarios and should not be taken as providing rules of general application.

It is also worth stressing that this is not a book concerned with claims for professional negligence by architects, although such claims form an important part of any discussion of fee recovery claims. Rather it is concerned with considering the steps which architects may take to avoid becoming involved in disputes over the payment of their fees; and where such disputes arise, the steps the architect may take to attempt to secure payment. Finally, it should be remembered that this book is *not* intended as a 'how to do it' guide to fee recovery. For specific problems, specialist advice should always be taken.

Introduction

The recurrent theme of this type of claim is that from the architect's perspective such claims are seldom straightforward: while only rarely raising complex legal issues, they are often complicated by uncertainties in the terms on which the architect was engaged; and they regularly feature clients who are tenacious in their desire not to pay.

Accordingly, the purpose of this book is to help practitioners avoid the situations which may give rise to claims, and to make the most of the 'damage limitation exercise' which occurs when disputes arise.

Endnote:

1 Luder, O. (2001) *A Guide to Keeping Out of Trouble*, London, RIBA Publications.

Getting Paid

1 An intractable problem

An artist or an administrator?

Claims by architects for payment of their fees raise a number of difficult problems. The nature of the architect's task is to translate the client's vision into a workable design and (in most forms of traditional contract) to administer the building process and deliver the finished product on time and within budget.

At every stage of this process there are potential pitfalls. Successful realisation of the project requires the combination of a number of disparate skills. In addition to the design of the works most projects involve the ability to use a variety of administrative skills which will include not only the day to day administration and co-ordination of the project but also the sometimes fraught business of managing the expectations of the client and acting as the main means of communication between the client and the contractor.

In a paper submitted to the *Building Design* seminar 'Fee Arrangements and Getting Paid' Oliver Richards of ORMS Architects put the matter precisely:

> I regard myself and my practice as forming part of the creative process. I find it frankly distasteful to talk about money.

He went on, however, to outline the practical necessity of addressing the issue of payment for services. The growing accent on the need to address issues such as profitability and the recovery of fees is a relatively new phenomenon. Traditionally, architecture had been regarded as a suitable job for a gentleman: a gentleman seldom quibbled about fees. Today, the sums at stake are often so large and the risks so great that even gentlemen architects have to collect their fees.

In the firing line

On many projects this inevitably means that the architect is the most obvious scapegoat when things go wrong. The term 'single point responsibility', favoured by many clients and intended to describe the situation where there is a single identifiable person or firm to whom all issues can be referred, is very easily translated into 'one person to blame'. The unique position occupied by the architect – on the one hand the representative of the client, and on the other, the administrator of the contract – means that in many contracts, the architect is particularly vulnerable. Even though in design and build contracts the traditional role of the architect, standing between client and contractor, has been diminished, the architect still holds a key position; after all, the parties are attempting to implement the designs the architect has produced and which comprise the employer's requirements.

From the client's viewpoint, it is tempting to attribute most problems to the architect. Regardless of whether the problems are actually the result of a failure by the architect, it is likely that the architect will encounter resistance in securing payment of fees. The client's rationale will often be that it had employed the architect to deliver the project: since the works did not accord with the client's expectations the architect should not have the fee. The perceived failures of the architect may take many forms but among the most common are:

- a failure to produce a design which reflects what the client actually wanted;
- a failure to administer the progress of the contractor, perhaps through obvious means such as the failure to issue instructions or design information, or less perceptibly, through the failure to ensure that the works proceeded at the pace allowed in the programme, or to enable the client to occupy the works by some particular date which may or may not have been communicated to the architect;
- a failure to produce a design capable of being constructed within the allowed budget;
- a failure to obtain planning consent;
- a failure to administer the works so as to ensure that they are constructed in accordance with the contract and free from obvious defects.

In some cases the client's concerns will be justified and there is a legitimate complaint which can be made against the architect. Those disputes are outside the scope of this book save with regard to the effect such claims have on fee collection.

Alternatively, it may simply be the case that the client has decided that it does not wish to pay the architect for his or her services; while others are unable to pay. This may be due to some premeditated act on the part of the client, or more commonly because, in the stressful atmosphere which pervades many projects, the relationship between client and architect has broken down.

Unfortunately, it is also sometimes the case that a client simply does not want to pay. The sums involved are often large and it may be tempting to evade payment. While there are no universally recognised distinguishing features for this type of client, the ability to spot them and avoid undertaking work on their behalf is likely to avoid difficulties at a later stage. Credit checks carried out on new clients at the beginning of a relationship can sometimes indicate potential problems.

An old axiom of practice is that it would be cheaper to write some potential clients a cheque for £10,000 when first approached than to accept their commission.

The uneven playing field

How does the architect secure payment of fees in such cases? The answer is often, 'with great difficulty'! Unfortunately, in many instances it has been (and sometimes still is) impossible for architects to pursue fee claims with realistic prospects of success. The reasons for this fall into three broad categories: administrative, economic and procedural.

Administrative factors

Administrative factors are considered in more detail in Chapter 2; as indicated above, the problem arises where the parties have failed to pay sufficient heed to finalising the terms on which the architect is to be retained: the services to be provided, the fees the architect is entitled to be paid (and when they are to be received) and the circumstances in which additional fees may be payable. In many cases this uncertainty only becomes apparent when the architect seeks to render a fee account, and the client seeks professional advice on whether it is obliged to pay it.[1]

Getting Paid

Since relatively few practices have either a credit controller or procedure in place where someone other than the job architect takes responsibility for chasing delinquent clients, this frequently brings the job architect into contact with his client: a calm, commercial approach becomes difficult.

This is often compounded by a failure to keep adequate records, or the absence of anything to confirm whether particular matters were actually agreed. The dispute becomes a question of one man's word against another's.

In such circumstances, while the consequences are often harsh, the architect will almost invariably be advised by a lawyer that claims in respect of fees will be difficult to sustain.

Economic factors

The average size of an architects' practice in Great Britain is between two and three people. The average turnover is perhaps £100,000. Even relatively substantial practices will be of modest size and resources compared with most commercial, and many private, clients. This inequality of bargaining position not only means that many practices conclude bad bargains (which as will be shown are more likely to result in disputes) but are often without the time or the resources to pursue their entitlement through the courts or arbitration. The inherent uncertainty of these processes and the risk that if unsuccessful the losing party will be responsible for not only their own costs but those of the winner mean that this is a gamble which few will be prepared to take. This risk is accentuated because, while the sum at stake means that it is highly material to the architect in terms of fee income in a given year, it will often be extremely small compared with the legal costs necessary to collect it.

Even if an architect successfully sues a client he or she may face difficulties in obtaining payment, particularly if the client is financially unsound, or is trading through an offshore company or a one-off special purpose company with no real assets. In these circumstances consideration should be given to advance payments.

Procedural factors

Prior to the Arbitration Act 1996, the Woolf Reforms and the right to mandatory adjudication provided by the Housing Grants, Construction and Regeneration Act (HGCRA) 1996, proceedings whether in the courts or through arbitration were almost always slow and labour-intensive. Even where it was possible to take advantage of the procedures allowing summary judgement or interim payments to be sought, such cases could still take several months to reach a hearing, with costs running into tens of thousands of pounds. Naturally, the time spent by the architect in assisting the legal team was time which could not be spent attending to fee-earning work.

However, the difficulties often faced in pursuing fee claims cannot be entirely attributed either to the iniquity of certain clients or the injustice of the legal system. In far too many cases the dispute arises from the architect's failure to attend to the very basic business of finalising his or her appointment. It is a truism that if the architect has not resolved precisely what he or she is supposed to do or the payment for doing it, it is more likely than not that a dispute will arise and that difficulties will inevitably occur in seeking to obtain payment.

It will therefore be readily appreciated that the three factors identified above need to be fully addressed. The following matters should be at the forefront of all architects' thinking:

- the need for increased rigor in the finalisation of appointments; an increased awareness of the terms and conditions to be incorporated into those appointments; and a greater precision in relation to payment terms – particularly in relation to excluding the client's rights of set-off;
- the availability of the means to pursue claims in respect of unpaid fees, particularly in relation to the availability of conditional fee agreements (CFAs) and appropriate legal expense insurance – to enable the architect to obtain the means to fund litigation or arbitration and to reduce the risk in the event that such claims are unsuccessful;
- the ability to use quick and efficient means of dispute resolution such as adjudication as a means of obtaining (at the very least) a rapid interim resolution of the dispute.

Getting Paid

The combination of the increasing awareness on the part of architects' practices of the importance of contractual issues, changes in the law and the evolution of standard forms of appointment, and the increased availability of both means of funding litigation and appropriately speedy remedies mean that the last five years have seen the tide turning in favour of architects.[2]

It is also worth remembering that help is at hand from an obvious but sometimes under-used source – the architect's professional indemnity insurers. It is sometimes overlooked that insurers not only have a vested interest in keeping their insured out of trouble but will have a large reservoir of practical experience to draw upon in order to assist their insured. The increasing sophistication of many professional indemnity insurers has led to many offering a range of assistance to their insured. This is considered in Chapter 6 as one of the tools available to architects.

Endnotes:

1 The recent decision in *Picardi* v *Cuniberti* makes it clear that a failure to finalise the terms of the appointment, and, as importantly, a failure to explain the terms of the appointment to the client will have potentially disastrous consequences.

2 Although the tide may be turning in favour of architects, care and vigilance are still called for, and the *Picardi* v *Cuniberti* case provides a timely illustration that nothing should be taken for granted.

2 The indemnity trap

Before looking at the steps which might be taken to improve the position of the architect it is worth looking at a relatively typical factual situation.[1]

Case Study 1

The works comprise the refurbishment of a large residential property in Central London. The client Ned is a wealthy businessman from overseas with no first-hand experience of UK construction. Part of the building is to be used as offices as the UK headquarters for the employer's business. The remainder is to form a luxury residence. The building contractor is a small specialist contractor of long-standing reputation and considerable experience in carrying out projects of this type.

A building contract is signed naming the architect Jim as contract administrator. Apparently 'for tax reasons' the employer under the building contract is named as an offshore one-off company, Ned Offshore Ltd. The client asks the architect to engage a professional team comprising a quantity surveyor, a structural engineer and a services engineer. Some uncertainty exists as to whether the professional team are to be employed by the client or as sub-consultants to the architect.

A series of discussions take place between Jim and Ned and a number of letters are written. Copies of the letters are in Appendix 1. The key points to note are as follows:

- a proposed fee is suggested based on a percentage of anticipated build cost. A counter proposal that 'I would prefer to agree a lump sum fee with you' does not receive a response;
- a meeting takes place at which the subject is discussed but this is not minuted save for a note in which the architect suggests that the terms of CE/95 be used and indicates 'if we are now going with the proposed alternative scheme we ought to do something in respect of the additional work required';

Getting Paid

> - a further meeting occurs which is minuted and is described as 'pre-start meeting' at which the subject of scope of services is addressed in terms which suggest that the issue is by no means settled.
>
> In fact the issue is not discussed beyond this point.

Before looking at the issues which will occur as the works get underway, it is worth pausing to consider the contractual position between the client and the architect. What exactly have they agreed, if anything?

The answer is far from clear. The question whether a contract has come into being will be measured by a four-stage test:[2]

- Do the parties intend that there should be a contract between them? Here the answer is yes.
- Have the parties agreed on all of the matters which the law regards as essential in order for a contract to come about? In general this will mean scope of works and price. Here the parties have most certainly not reached agreement on either scope of services or on the payment terms to be applied.[3]
- Have the parties agreed on everything which they regard as necessary in order for a contract to come into being? On the basis that the architect regards the incorporation of the terms of CE/95 as essential, again the answer is no.
- Have the parties evidenced their agreement in some way, principally by way of some written record or, in appropriate cases, by conduct? In this case they have not.

On the facts of Case Study 1, uncertainty affects both client and architect. For the architect Jim, it will be difficult to establish exactly what he is entitled to be paid and whether he is entitled to rely upon the protection afforded by the standard forms of appointment. For the client Ned, the difficulty is that he lacks certainty as to the services which the architect is required to provide.[4]

The indemnity trap

After their inauspicious start it is unsurprising that Ned and Jim experience a series of problems:

- difficulties are encountered with planning authorities over the change of use of part of the building;
- asbestos is discovered in existing ductwork which requires the suspension of work while it is removed. A lingering debate occurs as to whether this should have been picked up in the survey undertaken by the services consultant (and as to whether his work is the responsibility of the architect);
- delays occur in sourcing marble;
- the client issues instructions directly to the contractor which require the redesign of staircases and partitions;
- the client informs the architect and contractor that he requires to go into occupation of the works by his birthday – a date which would have predated the original completion date, but which, given the delays, now requires extensive acceleration to meet;
- the contractor submits a request for an extension of time and for additional payment in respect of delay, disruption and direct loss and expense. The architect is obliged to evaluate the application for an extension and to include any sum ascertained in respect of loss and expense in interim certificates.

Of these six occurrences only the last is something which the architect might have anticipated having to include within the scope of services – even assuming that the question of scope of services had been satisfactorily resolved. In respect of the remainder the architect is likely to be seeking some additional fee. Each of them will involve the architect in some measure of increased work.

Foreseeably, at the point when the architect attempts to raise the question of additional fees, the relationship with the client will be experiencing great strain. Faced with the situation where the project is running late and is over budget, the client may cast around for someone to blame and the architect's request for additional fees may represent the final straw – even where, as

Getting Paid

here, none of these matters can properly be said to be the fault of the architect.

In many instances, the effect of the architect's request for additional fees will be that, after a period of unsuccessful negotiation, the architect will threaten to take some steps to recover the fees. This will be met with a suggestion by the client that, far from the architect being entitled to further fees, the architect was in fact negligent in the performance of his or her duties. A counterclaim making a series of allegations will be submitted; while this may be impressive in terms of volume of allegations and size of claim, upon investigation it will often be seen to have little real substance.

Nonetheless, the architect prudently notifies his or her professional indemnity insurers. The insurers may well form the understandable view that while the claim appears ill-founded, the contractual arrangements between the parties are sufficiently uncertain that they should exercise caution. The legal costs of defending the claim are often so vast that the risks are not worth contemplating. The insurers may therefore take over conduct of the claim and counterclaim and conclude a deal with the client whereby the counterclaim is abandoned in exchange for a waiver of the claim for additional fees. For insurers this is obviously an appropriate deal to conclude – no payment is made under their policy and clearly no criticism can attach to them for so doing. However, the loser in these circumstances is the architect who loses the additional fees to which he or she would have been entitled. It would be unrealistic to suggest that insurers should fight the claim in these circumstances – they have little to gain from doing so. Equally, it would be folly for the architect not to notify.

This scenario has unfortunately proved all too common in recent years. Although it is quite possible for it to arise in circumstances where the architect had taken pains properly to conclude his or her appointment, all too often it arises where this has not been the case. While the failure to resolve contractual terms does not of itself give rise to problems it helps to ferment an atmosphere in which these problems become more likely to occur.

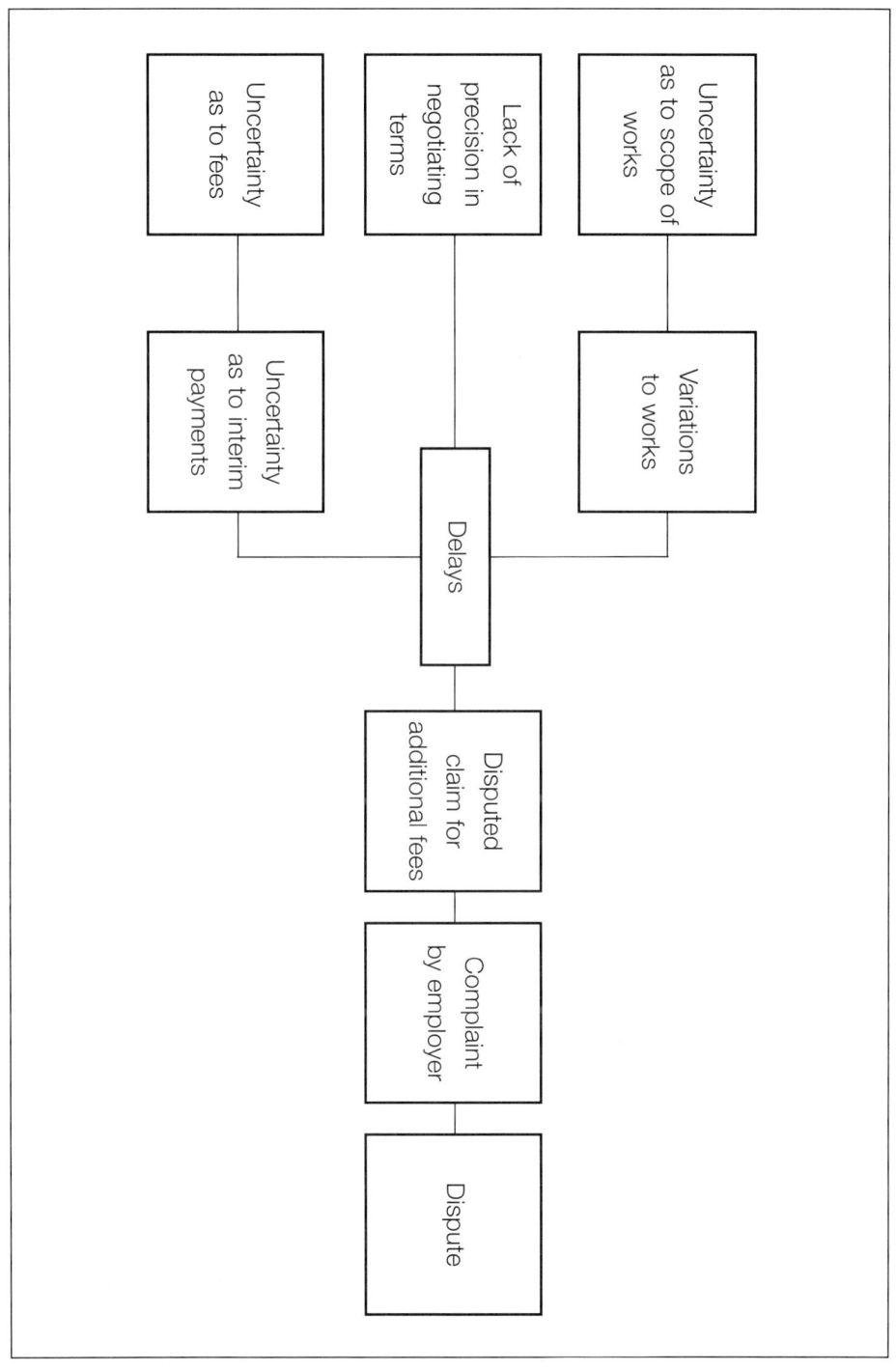

Figure 1: Development of a dispute

Getting Paid

From the architect's viewpoint a sense of disappointment is inevitable: a feeling that his or her fees have been 'sacrificed' in settling a claim with little merit. Looked at from the perspective of insurers the picture is clearer: if the contractual position of the insured is unclear to a degree where it is difficult to say with certainty what his or her obligations are, unless the claim is transparently hopeless it would be unwise of insurers to do anything but settle. Figure 1 (above) illustrates how these situations sometimes develop.

The late Raymond Cecil, long a respected columnist and a member of the RIBA Council, used to advise architects, 'every time you take an action, imagine you might have to justify it to a hostile barrister'; advice well worth bearing in mind.

Endnotes:

1. All the case studies in this book are based on elements from a number of 'real life' scenarios.
2. This test was set out in *Nuclear Civil Constructors* v *Atomic Power Constructions* [1962] 3 All ER 1035.
3. The same logic applies to the way the architect approached the work and particularly the job file. The importance of the latter in successfully pursuing a claim for payment can hardly be exaggerated. Not only should it contain clear and unambiguous written evidence of the terms on which the architect has accepted the commission, but all significant communications with the client and anyone else of importance in the project should be carefully recorded. This includes telephone conversations and meetings, which ideally should be confirmed to the people involved and if appropriate to the client. Care should be taken with each document to ensure it would be clear to a third party such as a judge or arbitrator, that it really says what was meant and says it in a way which will not cause embarrassment to the writer. Ideally, all file material should be made contemporaneously; if a note is written after the occurrence, the date on which it was written should be indicated. Particularly when dealing with private individuals, it would also be prudent to ensure that all of the important terms of the appointment have been explained – and there is a letter (or at least a file note) recording that the terms of the appointment have been explained.
4. Although the facts of the *Picardi* v *Cuniberti* (see above on p.8, and particularly p.119) are slightly different, the decision illustrates the unforgiving approach sometimes taken by the courts where the terms of an appointment are left to chance.

3 The right to payment

Before looking at the detailed machinery of architect's appointments it is worth looking briefly at the basis on which an architect is entitled to payment for work undertaken. The general rule, simply stated, is that where one party requests another to carry out work they are obliged to pay a reasonable sum for what is done; where the parties agree that certain work will be done for a certain price, that price will be what they are entitled to be paid.

Unsurprisingly, situations such as that described in the previous chapter mean that disputes over what precisely the architect is due to be paid are among the most common forms of disagreement. The lesson for the practitioner is clear – if nothing else, be sure about what has been agreed in respect of fees.

It is worth stressing that fees will be dictated by what the parties have actually agreed and (ideally) recorded in writing, and it will be difficult to go behind that agreement in all but the most exceptional circumstances.

Hence the following checklist, while probably not exhaustive, may be helpful:

- When am I entitled to be paid, and what?
- Am I entitled to deliver interim fee accounts, and if so, for how much?
- How long do I have to wait for invoices to be settled?
- Am I entitled to interest on late payments?
- Have I defined the circumstances in which I will be entitled to extra payment? Am I clear on exactly what is meant by extra – extra to what?
- If the work takes longer than I envisaged, am I entitled to an uplift to take account of inflation?
- What measures can I take if I am not paid – am I entitled to suspend performance or stop altogether?

The answers to some of these questions are provided by the HGCRA 1996 and Late Payment of Commercial Debts (Interest) Act 1998.

Housing Grants, Construction and Regeneration Act 1996

The important provisions of this Act are as follows:

- section 109: a party to a construction contract (as defined by the Act) is entitled to payments by installments unless the duration of the works is specified in the contract as being less than 45 days;
- section 110(1): every construction contract shall contain an adequate mechanism for determining stage payments and shall provide a mechanism for determining when any final payment shall become due;
- section 110(2): every construction contract shall provide for the giving of notice not later than five days after the date on which payment became due or would have become due if:
  (a) the other party had carried out his obligations under the contract; and
  (b) no set-off or abatement (see Chapter 5) was permitted by reference to sums otherwise due specifying the amount of the payment proposed to be made and the basis for its calculation;
- section 111: a party to a construction contract may not withhold payment unless he has given effective notice of his intention to do so, and that notice (which may be the same as the notice given under section 110(2)) must specify the grounds on which payment is to be withheld and the amount proposed to be so withheld, and if there is more than one ground, each ground and that amount attributable to it;
- section 112: a party who has not been paid in accordance with the contract may suspend performance if following the giving of seven days' notice payment has not been made, provided no valid withholding notice has been served;
- section 113: a provision making payment conditional upon receiving payment from another party shall be ineffective save where the third party is insolvent;
- where the contract in question does not contain the machinery prescribed by sections 109 and 110, the default mechanisms specified by the Scheme for Construction Contracts shall apply.[1]

The right to payment

Accordingly, the first three questions in the checklist set out above are addressed under the HGCRA 1996 and the fourth is dealt with under the Late Payment of Commercial Debts (Interest) Act 1998.

Although these matters will be incorporated into the contract between architect and client by operation of law, it makes sense to ensure that they are brought to the attention of the client and clearly understood by the client – there will be circumstances in which the above Acts will not apply, and there may be instances where their application is arguable, hence it is sensible to ensure that these points are resolved.[2]

While the ARB Standards of Conduct require the agreement between the architect and the client to be in writing, there is surprisingly no specific RIBA practice guidance dealing with in how much detail an architect should explain the appointment agreement to the client. Common sense suggests the architect should err on the side of safety and over-explain, particularly with regard to first time or lay clients. In relation to the latter, the Unfair Contract Terms Act 1977 requires the architect to act reasonably and not to impose onerous terms.

Developing the point touched on in the previous chapter, there are a number of circumstances in which uncertainty over fees can arise unless dealt with at the outset. Unfortunately there are also a number of scenarios in which such disputes can arise despite the architect's best efforts to achieve certainty. Both are dealt with at p.37 and in respect of both types of situation the expression most commonly used by architects when seeking subsequent legal advice is 'we didn't see it coming'. Although both concern circumstances in which additional fees are payable, it will be noted that disputes over additional fees emanate from uncertainty over what is included within the architect's basic fee.

Getting Paid

Uncertainty in the appointment

It is not uncommon to encounter situations where the parties have agreed the fees which are to be payable but where the works alter or tasks are required for which no provision is made in the fee agreement. As will be seen at p.37, where the parties have agreed that one of the standard forms of appointment is to be used this is unlikely to be a problem; the standard forms contain provisions for payment for additional or varied work.

What happens, however, where this is not the case? It is worth remembering that the mere fact that a standard form has been referred to in correspondence is no guarantee that its terms will be incorporated into the contract between the parties.

> **Scenario 1**
> I will do the initial design, submit the planning application and liaise with the quantity surveyor in relation to the obtaining of tenders and appointment of the contractor. I will then act as supervising officer over the works and you will pay me £x.

The employer agrees but later instructs the architect to design a new wing to the property. There is no provision for variations to the architect's scope of services. However, it is probable that in this situation the architect will be able to say that the scope of services was finite and that this comprised an extra for which he or she is entitled to payment. That payment is probably to be calculated on the basis of a reasonable sum. The starting point for calculation of this sum is likely to be the architect's hourly rates, although this is not conclusive.

> **Scenario 2**
> I will oversee the works comprising the design and supervision of the project in return for a fee of £y.

Again the employer agrees. At the time the parties both envisage that the works will comprise a particular scheme with a clear budget. Unfortunately as the works progress, additional design works and additional attendance becomes necessary as the size of the project grows. Is the architect entitled to

The right to payment

additional payment in respect of the work over and above that which was anticipated? The answer is probably not.

There is no doubt that the architect has carried out more work than was originally envisaged. However, it will be argued by the employer that on a proper view the architect had agreed to do everything necessary to complete the design and supervision of the works. In other words, the architect had assumed the risk of extra work being required.

The distinction between the two scenarios lies in the words used rather than in the practical results achieved. In the first the architect has succeeded in specifying the services they are to provide. In the second the architect has specified the result they are to accomplish. The crucial difference is that in the first, it is possible to say that specific tasks will be performed, and that when they have been undertaken, the architect has no further obligations. If required to do more, the architect is entitled to additional payment. By contrast, the second situation is really akin to a performance specification. There is no limitation on the work required to produce a particular result.

It goes without saying that the second scenario produces a result which is harsh. However it is important to dispel the myth that extra work automatically gives rise to a right to extra payment. The moral is quite clear: wherever possible every effort should be made to ensure that the scope of works to be undertaken is defined in precise terms. The RIBA standard forms of agreements, for example, SFA/99 (updated April 2000) sets out in Schedule 2: Services the common tasks that the architect will perform (amended if appropriate) as defined in the RIBA Plan of Work and described in various RIBA Enterprises' publications such as the *Architect's Job Book*[3].

Getting Paid

Uncertainties arising in the course of the works

All too often circumstances will arise where the architect is required to undertake works which were not envisaged at the time the appointment was concluded, but where disputes arise as to whether the architect is entitled to additional payment.

Clause 5.6 of SFA/99 provides a typical example of a clause governing the right to additional payment:

> If the Architect, for reasons beyond his control is involved in extra work or incurs extra expense, for which he will not otherwise be remunerated, the Architect shall be entitled to additional fees calculated on a time basis unless otherwise agreed. Reasons for such entitlement include, but shall not be limited to:
>
> 1 the scope of the Services or the Timetable or the period specified for any work stage is varied by the Client;
>
> 2 the nature of the Project requires that substantial parts of the design cannot be completed or must be specified provisionally or approximately before construction commences;
>
> 3 the Architect being required to vary any item of work commenced or completed pursuant to the Agreement or to provide a new design after the Client has authorised the Architect to develop an approved design;
>
> 4 delay or disruption by others;
>
> 5 prolongation of any building contract(s) relating to the Project;
>
> 6 the Architect consenting to enter into any third party agreement the form or beneficiary of which had not been agreed by the Architect at the date of the Agreement;

The right to payment

7 the cost of any work designed by the Architect or the cost of special equipment is excluded from the Construction Cost.

This clause 5.6 shall not apply where the extra work and/or expense to which it refers is due to a breach of the Agreement by the Architect.[4]

There is clearly scope for argument over what is a delay beyond the control of the architect. Obviously it is difficult to draft provisions to cover circumstances not envisaged by the parties at the time they contracted. It is impossible to produce a comprehensive wording to cover those factual scenarios which do arise through no fault of the architect, and those which do not, since this will depend on the particular facts which prevail on the specific job. While there is room for semantic debate, the task for the architect is to show as a minimum requirement that:

- they have undertaken extra work – it follows from the preceding section that this does not simply mean more work than the architect expected;
- the extra work was not necessitated by an act of or omission by the architect.

Among the arguments which the architect may face will be the following:

- while the works were additional, and arose through no fault of the architect, they should have been foreseen by the architect and thus should have been included within the architect's fee;
- the client's variation did not involve the architect in extra work or if it did it was in order to ensure that the architect actually fulfilled the original design brief which otherwise they would not have done;
- that in fact the delay or additional work arose as a consequence of some default on the part of the architect.

The last of these is the most frequently encountered reason for disputes over fees. Superficially this is something which might occur however carefully the parties have negotiated the terms of their appointment. At first glance, it is a consequence of the way in which the architect carries out the services as

Getting Paid

opposed to the terms agreed for their performance. However, there is no doubt that the architect's best chance of avoiding disputes is where his or her appointment has been carefully and comprehensively worked out. Uncertainty over what the architect is supposed to do, or confusion over the terms of payment will increase the prospects of the client considering that it has not received that which it had expected. Hence the next chapter looks in detail at the terms of architects' appointments.

The checklist at Appendix 2 provides indications of the pitfalls which await the unwary. What is more serious is the fact that the courts will look at what the parties have actually agreed, rather than what they might have intended. Indeed, in construing an agreement, English law will give the words actually used their ordinary everyday meaning and will have no regard to the intentions of the parties.[5]

Perhaps most significantly, there is no requirement of reasonableness in English law. Although it might be said that what is reasonable for one party may be unreasonable for the other, if the parties have agreed something which is onerous for one or both of them, the courts will give effect to it. Put another way, if the parties have agreed a nonsense, a nonsense is what they will have.

It is not uncommon for architects to be engaged on the basis that they will initially be paid on an hourly rate while discussions take place as to the precise scope of the works, and once the building contract is finalised and a lump sum is agreed this is converted into a percentage of the eventual build cost. Indeed, as will be seen in Chapter 4, this approach is specifically envisaged in the standard forms of appointment.

In most instances this approach works satisfactorily, and of course it has been widely used for many years. There are, however, circumstances where it can lead to problems. Problems arise for two reasons: first the delay in finalising the scope of the works and secondly the uncertainty as to the sums which will be due to the contractor. Often – and sometimes with some justification – the client perceives that the extended process of design development leading to the finalisation of the works is being carried out at its cost and on a trial and error basis. The response to this – which may be equally justified – is that in a refurbishment project where much of the work proceeds on the basis of reacting to situations as they are discovered, there will always be an extent to which the works are designed as a response to dimensions and conditions which may be encountered.

The simple answer is that this approach to fee calculation may not be appropriate to projects which are to be let on either a prime cost basis or where a significant amount of design information is still awaited at the time the contract is let, especially where it is envisaged that much of this information may only become available as the project progresses. In these circumstances, a more flexible approach in which remuneration is geared towards the works actually undertaken may be more apt.

The clear lesson is that there is considerable risk in committing to any form of fixed or capped fee where the works to be included within that fee are incapable of precise ascertainment. A distinction may perhaps be drawn here between the risk of design development, and the risk that an entire stratum of work which had not been foreseen at the outset may be encountered. With the former the architect is largely in control of their own fate. The architect's skill in pricing the costs of designing the works is to gauge the amount of time they may have to spend in honing their design. With the latter, the architect is being asked to price the unknowable. A common theme is that where the architect has sought to be paid as an extra for works which the client contended fell within the original brief, problems inevitably arise.[6]

The moral is clear: the architect should think carefully about what will occur if the works change or extras are required. Is extra payment going to result, and if so, by what means has it been ensured that this is the case? Do not make the mistake of assuming either that additional work necessarily means an additional fee, or that an additional fee will be available simply because it would be unfair not to be paid extra.

Case Study 2 illustrates some of the difficulties which may arise in this sort of situation.

Getting Paid

Case Study 2

Albert is an architect who has recently commenced his own practice. Bernard is a long-standing social acquaintance. Until recently Bernard worked for a firm of commercial property agents, but has recently been 'head-hunted' to lead a consortium who wish to develop a city centre site. Discussions begin between Albert and Bernard with a view to Albert acting as architect for the project. Some initial site arrangement drawings are produced. A lengthy period elapses during which the scene takes shape and Bernard negotiates independently with his backers to obtain funding. Throughout this period Bernard makes it clear that the 'budget is tight' without defining exactly what this is intended to mean. Eventually he makes it known that the scheme can go ahead. By this time Albert has been working for several months on a speculative basis.

Albert writes a letter the key parts of which read:

> I am pleased that matters seem to be sorted out with your backers and we can now proceed. We probably need to talk about fees, terms and the like. I enclose a copy of the latest version of the RIBA form which is commonly used on jobs of this sort.
>
> If we were proceeding on the basis of scale rates I would be proposing a fee which would equate to something of the order of £125,000. In the circumstances I think it would be appropriate to reduce this and I suggest:
>
> £10,000 up to submission of planning application
> £10,000 for production of detailed design
> £10,000 overseeing tender applications and negotiating with tenderers where appropriate
> £20,000 works on site
>
> Total £50,000.

The right to payment

Bernard replies 'I accept your fee proposal of £50,000'.

Shortly after this date, Bernard tells Albert that he has pre-let the majority of the premises and to avoid an extension of the rent-free period, the works need to be practically complete by a date some six months hence. A discussion occurs and Albert's day-book notes agreement that while tight this date was considered achievable 'if no major snags are encountered'.

Tenders are sought and prove greater than anticipated. After some negotiation and attendant delay a compromise is reached and the building contract is signed.

Works commence and proceed for some months. A range of problems occur which fall into three main categories:

- problems with planning and building regulations. While foreseen at the time of the original agreement these prove significantly more severe than anticipated. It is accepted by Albert and Bernard that these are not anyone's fault but nonetheless they have the effect of causing serious delays;
- the contractor fails to perform. Late in the contract period he starts to write letters suggesting this may have been due to late supply of information;
- a range of variations are ordered. In some cases this is done by way of direct instructions from Bernard. He also negotiates directly with the contractor to remove two major packages from the contract, the decoration and the raised floors and lets them directly to the trade contractors. In an ambiguous site-meeting minute it is suggested that this is done with Albert's approval in order to 'accelerate' the works although Albert's recollection is that the first he knew of this was when he was told that this had been done. This causes further major delays.

Getting Paid

> The result is extensive delay, increases in the tenant's rent-free period, a substantial variations account and a large, although undetailed, claim from the contractor. Unsurprisingly Albert finds that having calculated his price on the basis of an estimated number of hours which would be required to perform his services, this has been greatly exceeded. In some instances he can point to specific instructions to do particular pieces of additional work. In others he simply finds that the work required has increased massively.
>
> Accordingly he writes to Bernard suggesting that the scope of the work has increased greatly and this should be reflected in his fees. He suggests:
>
>> If I approached the matter on a strict basis I consider I would be entitled to something like a further £100,000, but propose we compromise at a further £75,000 which I believe is a fair reflection of what I have put into the project.
>
> After a reminder, Bernard writes back stating that they had agreed an all-in price of £50,000 and this was what he was going to pay 'particularly in view of the problems for which you must bear responsibility as my architect'.

The problem for Albert is easier to state than it is to answer. Whether by accident or design, Bernard has placed Alfred in a position where he has spent so much time on the project that he is committed to it proceeding and almost any fee is better than none. Additionally, when fees have been discussed, while both parties thought that what they had agreed was clear – and Bernard's approach can certainly be accused of being sharp – there is an unquestionable ambiguity as to what they have actually agreed. On one view, Alfred has committed himself to a lump sum for the project.

The lessons are equally clear. While speculative work is a part of the working life of most architects, it is important wherever possible to identify clear limits and to attempt to strike a balance in the workload of a practice between 'developmental' projects where work is being carried out speculatively and 'non-speculative' projects where fee-earning work is being carried out. Necessarily, this is a counsel of perfection but it is important for architects, like any other business, to appreciate that tomorrow's big job will not pay the bills.

The further lesson is that certainty with regard to fee arrangements cannot be valued too highly. It is simply not enough to say that the parties thought they understood what was being agreed if one of them can argue plausibly that the plain words used could be construed to mean something different. Neither does it help to suggest that by seeking to contend something other than 'what we agreed' the client is behaving unreasonably or unfairly. Although the client may indeed be behaving unreasonably, as we have seen, this is not a route to a legal remedy.

It is also important for the architect to highlight the need for additional work before the architect carries it out and to explain to the client why this has occurred. Although nobody wants to learn about additional cost, most clients will be happier to hear this before the cost is incurred than after. Also the architect will be in a far stronger position if the client has not already had the benefit of the work for which the architect requires additional fees. A practice long prevalent in the United States which is becoming more common in Britain is for the architect to issue a form of 'design instruction' to the client whenever the need for additional design work becomes apparent (similar to an architect's instruction issued to the contractor during the course of construction) informing the client of the need for additional work, what caused it, the amount of the additional fee cost (if possible) and noting the terms of the design contract under which additional fees are justified. A client in receipt of such a form before the design work is carried out will find it more difficult to argue later that it should not pay any additional sums requested.

Getting Paid

As with proposing contract forms to new clients, architects are often reluctant to raise the issue of additional work for fear of irritating the client. Before taking the path of least resistance, they should contemplate whether, at the end of the day, they will feel happier if the discussions with the client regarding these matters had been held before or after they spent the time and resources in carrying out work.

Endnotes:

1. The Scheme for Construction Contracts (1996) provides default mechanisms for interim payments – see also p.113.

2. Once again the decision in *Picardi* v *Cuniberti* is instructive (see below p.119). The Judge stressed the importance of explaining the terms of the appointment, noting that the burden of proving that the terms had been explained rested with the architect, and quoting with approval the comments of Lord Denning in an earlier case that some clauses would need 'to be printed in red ink on the face of the document, with a red hand pointing to it.'

3. Lupton, S. (Ed.) (2002) *Architect's Job Book Seventh Edition*, London, RIBA Enterprises.

4. The other commonly used standard forms of appointment are in substantially the same terms.

5. There are limited exceptions to this proposition, which are largely outside the scope of this work. In general, they are likely to arise in circumstances where the agreement reached fails to reflect what was meant by both parties, rather than where one party has entered into an agreement the effects of which are harmful or prejudicial to them. And remember that the burden of proving what was agreed will generally rest with the architect.

6. An interesting parallel is provided by the use in certain design and build contracts of so-called 'guaranteed maximum price' agreements. This expression is something of a misnomer, and while the form of these agreements differ, they share a common feature, namely that they tend to be used where the employer wishes to fix the contractor with responsibility for design development. Architects working for contractors on a project where the contractor has entered into such a contract with the employer should be reluctant to accept similar terms.

4 Appointments

Contractual relations

The relationship between the architect and the client is a contractual one. In the simplest terms a contract for architectural services comprises an agreement, whether by words, writing, conduct, or a combination of all three, whereby the architect agrees to perform services in exchange for payment. A contract comes into being when one party makes an offer which the other accepts. This can be as simple as a client saying 'please design a house for me, and I will pay you for what you do' to which the architect says 'yes'.[1]

In such circumstances, the architect is entitled to payment for the work done, and in the absence of a written agreement, the entitlement will be to a reasonable sum. The parties can agree that the works can be terminated at any time without either incurring any penalty.

Of course, this sort of open-ended agreement will only be suitable for the simplest arrangements. In particular, parties usually find it desirable to identify precisely the work to be undertaken or the services to be performed, and the payments to be made in respect of the services, generally broken down to allow stage payments to be made as particular milestones are reached, or specific services are performed. This has led to the evolution of standard forms of Architect's Appointment.

In 1971, RIBA published *Conditions of Engagement* (the 'Purple Book') which set out terms on which the architect was to be employed including the scope of work, remuneration (set out as a non-negotiable fee scale), and other matters. This was superseded in 1982 by *Architect's Appointment* (the 'Blue Book') which elaborated on its predecessor but, after scale fees had been attacked by the Office of Fair Trading, substituted a recommended fee graph for the earlier fee scales.

In 1992, the first of the current series of architects' agreements was issued, the 'Standard Form of Agreement for the Appointment of an Architect' (SFA/92) which was more comprehensive than the previous forms. Notable amongst the many new terms included for the first time were the right of the architect to suspend work for non-payment of fees (clause 1.6.3) and a prohibition against

Getting Paid

set-off (clause 1.5.15). Variations of or supplements to this form were introduced to deal with design and build, historic buildings and other non-traditional cases. CE/95 was later introduced with the same terms but to be used with a letter of appointment. A small works form was also brought in (SW/96) but is outside the scope of this book as its terms do not offer the protections of the other forms and so should be used for only the smallest of jobs.

Recently, the series was updated and is now published as SFA/99. The April 2000 edition in particular includes a number of clauses which will be of invaluable assistance to an architect seeking a payment which is being unreasonably withheld:

- clause 5.11: the proscription against set-off is retained from SFA/92;
- clause 5.13: late payment will attract interest at a rate of 8 per cent over base rate in line with the Late Payment of Commercial Debts (Interest) Act 1998;
- clause 9.2: following the enactment of the HGCRA 1996, adjudication is provided as a way of settling disputes but with the express proviso that the adjudicator may award costs;
- clause 9.5.3: an arbitrator under SFA/99 or CE/99 cannot award security for costs (it should be noted that arbitration is the method of dispute resolution for all sums over £5,000 where this agreement is used; although many solicitors prefer litigation, arbitration was specified as the courts cannot be directed not to award security for costs);
- clause 9.6: the client must indemnify the architect in respect of their legal and other costs together with a reasonable sum in respect of their time spent if the architect obtains a judgement in his or her favour.

The last of these is particularly important as it means that all the time reasonably spent by the architect in chasing a bad debt can be claimed against the client. It also means that the architect does not recover just 'assessed' legal costs (usually about two-thirds of the total) from the client in a successful fee recovery but nearly all.

The second part of this clause 'or 2. the Client fails to obtain a judgement for any claim or any part of any claim against the Architect' is designed to discourage a client from mounting a 'fishing expedition' against the architect by alleging a long list of doubtful or even vexatious negligence claims against an architect in an attempt to cause their insurers' lawyers to have to spend so much time and cost in defending against them that they require the architect to settle the claim with his or her fees unpaid. Taken literally, a client mounting such a claim will have to succeed on all parts of the claim in order not to be liable for the architect's full, indemnity costs as well as its own. In practice this is likely to be viewed by the courts as a question of degree. Nevertheless in times when professional indemnity insurance is becoming more expensive and difficult to obtain, this provision should help reduce the likelihood and amount of claims and attendant legal costs.

It may be useful for an architect, faced with what he or she considers to be a vexatious negligence counterclaim, to advise the client that, should it persist, the matter will be taken over by the architect's insurers (who will fund the action) and their specialist lawyers. The client might feel that it is about to take on more than it had bargained for and drop the claim.

Appointments with fear

The personal nature of the relationship between architect and client means that some architects find it difficult to broach the question of their appointment with their client. Indeed it is not uncommon to find experienced practitioners who regard it as an article of faith that the strength of their relationship with their client has avoided the need for the parties ever to conclude a formal document. However, any architect who is tempted to go down this path should imagine for a minute which they would prefer: to agree with a prospective client the details of scope of work, remuneration and the method of enforcing payment before they have expended the considerable time and expense of doing the work, or alternatively to do the work first, only to have the client dispute payment, leaving the architect financially exhausted, in a position where the practice is threatened and ill-prepared to devote the time and resources to pursuing the client for the fees due.[2]

Getting Paid

Architects are often drawn into doing speculative work for clients. This usually means that the architect carries out preliminary design work in return for being awarded the commission if some event occurs, such as the obtaining of finance for the project or the grant of planning permission. All too often it is never agreed how much work will be done on a speculative basis nor the terms on which the architect is eventually to be appointed. Too often there is a failure to appreciate that having a contract before starting speculative work is just as important as in more conventional commissions. Such a contract should not only spell out the terms of the architect's appointment once the project is to proceed on a firm basis, but also precisely what services the architect is supplying speculatively and what event triggers the implementation of the employment of the architect on a firm basis. Architects would be well advised to ensure that in such agreements the client's right to suspend or terminate the architect's commission (clauses 8.1 and 8.5 in SFA/99) be omitted.

Naturally, the problem with this attitude is that when problems do arise they are likely to be more serious by reason of the failure to finalise the terms on which the architect has been appointed. The message of the previous chapter is that concluded appointments will not prevent disputes, but since a high proportion of disputes arise out of uncertainty in relation to the terms on which works were to be carried out or the scope of services to be provided they represent a step in the right direction.

This part of the chapter considers the process of concluding an appointment and the material terms of the most commonly used standard forms of appointment, as well as a more general look at the pros and cons of some of the 'made to measure' appointment documents favoured by some developers.

Some architects are reluctant to discuss properly the terms of their appointment with a client. They are keen to get on with the project and perhaps feel that it will put the client off. They harbour the twin notions that to explain the terms of the appointment risks boring the client, and that to be 'too contractual' is to ask for trouble. However, the sensible client will be pleased to learn what its commitment is and what the architect will be doing for their remuneration. An interesting comparison is with solicitors' obligations at the

Appointments

start of a retainer to set out in detail the precise terms of their retainer.

At the start of a relationship, the client is choosing the architect presumably because the client thinks highly of them or has had the architect recommended (unless the architect is being chosen merely on the basis that they are cheapest) and so there is no better time for the architect to raise matters of terms and payment. The architect can say with some justification that their profession goes further than any other in setting out in writing just what they will do and how they will charge, although by contrast with solicitors, there is no sanction if the architect does not. Most clients are unaware of all the tasks an architect performs in the course of carrying out even the smallest of jobs.

A comprehensive list of these tasks is provided in Ray Moxley's somewhat out of date *The Architect's Guide to Fee Negotiations* and Richard Byrom's *Terms of Engagement and Fees*.[3] If the client is going to prove difficult about such matters, then perhaps it is better that the architect is forewarned and can consider withdrawing before any great resources are committed to the project.

Architects should take some time to describe the key points of the agreement to the client, particularly if they have not been involved in the building process before.[4] The fact that the architect has given a detailed description should be noted in the file, as it will do no harm in a fee recovery action to be able to say in court that they have done so. (As with so many things, if the architect looks after the client's interests, his or her own interests are looked after as well.) The architect should not be afraid of negotiation, although all but superficial amendments to the terms should be put to the architect's solicitor or professional indemnity insurer. After all, the single most important issue for the architect will be whether any of the terms on which they are being asked to act offend against the terms of their insurance cover. Experience suggests that the client who takes care to negotiate an agreement is more likely to honour it – it is the clients who accept an agreement without question who seem more likely to raise difficulties at a later date.

Getting Paid

Architects often find that they send an agreement to a prospective client who 'forgets' to return it signed. The architect is reluctant to press for a signature for fear of putting off the client before the job has started. Whilst a signed contract is indisputable evidence that a client has agreed to its terms, where the client has not objected to the terms of a contract presented to it and has continued to allow work to proceed, the courts will generally deem that it has accepted its terms by its conduct provided there is some evidence that the client has actually accepted the terms of the appointment. However, it is essential in such cases that there is good evidence that the client did receive the proposed agreement and the architect explained its terms to the client. It should be handed by the architect to the client (and so noted in the file) or sent by recorded delivery. The fact that the terms were explained should be confirmed in writing. All the architect's invoices should say 'in accordance with the agreement between us dated ...' which, when they are paid, will act as further evidence that the client has accepted the terms.

A number of the terms in an architect–client agreement will relate directly to remuneration. Using SFA/99 as an example, those usually of most importance to both parties are set out in Schedule 3, Fees and Expenses, where the basis of charging fees, expenses and disbursements are set out (see at p.38). Whilst the various methods of calculating fees are not the subject of this book, it is worth mentioning that the hourly rates should be carefully considered.

Most projects throw up work for the architect additional to what was originally expected and these rates are usually the basis on which this additional work is charged for (see also p.38). However, a number of the terms in the Conditions of Engagement relate also to remuneration, particularly those under section 5, Payment. These should be explained with particular care. Most important is clause 5.6, Additional Fees, which is discussed in Chapter 3. It is wise to make the client aware from the beginning of the general principle that additional work for the architect will attract an additional fee, in order to avoid the list of problems discussed in Chapter 3. If the architect is aware that a special class of additional work is likely to arise, they would be well advised to include it explicitly in Schedule 3, Time Charge Fees.

Appointments

Attention should also be drawn to clause 5.10. This stipulates that fees are due within 30 days and no more frequently than at one month intervals (subject to anything said in Schedule 3, Installments). One of the best ways an architect has of reducing his or her exposure to bad debts is by billing often and ensuring that bills are paid promptly. Not only does this sustain the architect's cash flow, it reduces the amount to be billed later. This, if left at too large a sum, can tempt unscrupulous clients into resisting payment, particularly when the architect may have finished the work that was needed. In cash flow terms, late payment and non payment are often much the same. However, in many instances the architect has only himself or herself to blame by allowing a large sum of work in progress to build up.

The descriptions of the scope of work refer to tasks, well known by architects at least, which are defined in the RIBA Plan of Work and described in RIBA Enterprises' publications such as *Architect's Job Book*[5].

The architect should take care to specify as precisely as possible the services to be performed. Not only should they carefully complete Schedule 2, Services, if applicable they should strike out or add to the Services Supplement. The architect should remember that they will have to carry out for their normal fee all the services in the schedule and supplement.

The architect will use the most recent evidence of the construction cost in pricing the services, normally first the client's budget, then the latest quantity surveyor's estimate(s), then the lowest acceptable tender, then the latest of the quantity surveyor's periodic financial reports as the construction progresses, then last the final account to base the interim fees on, interpolating as necessary between estimated construction costs and work stages. It is conceivable that, if the quantity surveyor has badly over-estimated the construction cost before tender, the architect may have to refund the 'excess' fee to the client and complete the last stages for nothing.

The architect should carefully complete Schedule 3, Fees and Expenses, as this provides the mechanism for reimbursement. Each section on fees, expenses and disbursements and installments should be set out in detail so

Getting Paid

that it is clear what payment is due and when. An example might be:

Work Stage Fees
Fee for Work Stage C Outline Proposals to Work Stage L After Practical Completion inclusive as scheduled in the Services Supplement to be calculated at 6% of the Construction Cost.

Time Charge Fees
Additional services, for example, interior design, on a time charge basis.

Expenses
Expenses and disbursements including travelling, subsistence, printing, copies, etc will be charged at cost plus a handling charge of 20%.

Installments
Fees, disbursements and expenses: interim payments monthly subject to the following stage payments (together with any time charges accruing) for Stages C through L:

- Outline Proposals (stage C): 15%
- Detailed Proposals (stage D): a further 20%
- Final Proposals (stage E): a further 20%
- Production Information (stage F): a further 20%
- Tender Documentation and Tender Action (stages G and H): a further 5%
- Mobilisation and Construction to Practical Completion (stages J and K): a further 17.5%

A total of 97.5% to be paid before the Architect issues the Certificate of Practical Completion
After Practical Completion (stage L): a further 2.5%

Total: 100%

(Note in the above example the requirement that the architect be paid most of his or her fee before the issuance of the Certificate of Practical Completion.

Commercial clients often need this certificate to release funds and are less likely to quibble with architects about fees if this condition is included. The wise architect will have formulated their claim for any additional work before submitting his or her fee at this point.)

(Note also that the percentages used in the above example are similar to those set out in the Blue and Purple Books before the Office of Fair Trading discouraged this. They are a good indication of the proportion of work for each stage on many jobs. Architects should be wary of clients who wish to alter these percentages in the preliminary stages in order substantially to defer fees.)

SFA/99 envisages that the parties should fill in the printed booklet and execute it at the end; CE/99 anticipates the use of a letter of appointment substantially in the form of the draft annexed. Subject to the proviso above about ensuring the client is deemed to have received and accepted the agreement, either method is perfectly appropriate.

However, some less satisfactory shortcuts include the following:[6]

- 'the terms will be the same as those on the last job';
- 'the appointment will incorporate the latest standard form';
- 'on the terms on which X carried out his contract with Y'; or
- 'on the terms recommended by the RIBA'.

The danger with shortcuts

There are obviously other forms of words used and this is not by any means an inclusive list. Even where both parties believe that they know what is intended by this sort of expression, this approach leaves hostages to fortune. Stating the obvious, these shortcuts have two major drawbacks. The first is that even if each party believes they know precisely what the words used are intended to mean, each party may mean something slightly different and the lack of precision about exactly what is meant may mean that when disagreements arise they are difficult to resolve. The second is that even if it is possible to identify the particular terms and conditions, because the parties have not sought to tailor the relevant appointment to the needs of the project in hand it is possible that there will be gaps or mismatches where either particular

Getting Paid

circumstances are not dealt with at all or they are dealt with in a manner which is inappropriate to the present project.

Common sense suggests in these circumstances that the parties should ask themselves whether what they have written down actually reflects the agreement between them.

This sort of situation is not helped by the rather puritanical approach adopted by the law to the interpretation of contracts, which has been touched upon in the previous chapter. The following points are worth stressing.

- It is unwise to assume that a particular state of affairs exists, or an agreement has been reached unless this is carefully confirmed in writing – see *Picardi* v *Cuniberti* for a salutary lesson of what can go awry when matters are left to chance.
- The courts will not undo bad bargains. Even if the parties have agreed something which is plainly silly, the courts will not rewrite the agreement except in extreme cases.
- The concepts of reasonableness and good faith have very limited application in English law. The circumstances in which the court will intervene in a contract which is said to be 'unreasonable' or even where one party might be said to be acting in bad faith are extremely restricted.
- Hence the fact that one party might have acted in good faith on the reasonable (but wrong) assumption that a particular state of affairs existed will not assist them unless they fall within one of the very limited exceptions.[7]
- The belief that in some way absences or inconsistencies can be made good by implied terms is mistaken. As a general rule the courts will give the agreement literal effect. Only if a term is necessary to give effect to the contract and if it is not inconsistent with the express terms of the contract will the courts consider implying terms.
- A contract will be construed by reference to its ordinary everyday meaning and the courts will have regard to the words used by the parties. The fact that the parties intended that the words used would have some other meaning will not be relevant unless this is clear from the face of the document. Extraneous evidence of the intention of the parties will not be admissible.

Appointments

- The argument that a contract can be re-written because it was procured by duress is also unlikely to be successful. Although the concept of 'equality of arms' is espoused by the Human Rights Act 1998, the courts have already given indications the arguments based on the Act are to be confined to the abuse of human rights and are not to be added to the list of arguments used to try to go behind commercial agreements.[6]

It follows that as a general proposition the advantages in properly concluding a form of appointment vastly outweigh any perceived disadvantages in adopting a 'contractual' approach.[9]

Case Study 3 illustrates some of the difficulties discussed above.

Case Study 3

Charles is an architect who is asked by Desmond, a wealthy businessman, to design and oversee refurbishment works to his house. Desmond has already engaged a contractor and Charles plays little part in the negotiation of terms with the contractor, save that he is made aware by Desmond when first contacted that the building contract, while notionally let on the basis of a lump sum, contains a large number of prime cost and provisional sum items. In large part, Charles's failure to do this is because Desmond tells him that he has engaged a firm of project managers who will 'look after that side of things'.

In fact, Desmond's comments are inaccurate if not actually untrue. Desmond is extremely anxious to start work and therefore soon after Charles is engaged he asks that works should start, at a time when Charles's design works have not proceeded much beyond outline designs. The scope of the works is far from settled.

Accordingly, in the early stages the works proceed on what is essentially a prime cost basis. Charles's drawings and details are produced on an increasingly ad hoc basis to cope with the progress of the works, and predictably any concept of a programme is rapidly abandoned in favour of progressing as well and as fast as the slowest part of the design and construction process admits.

Getting Paid

Nevertheless, Charles produces a fee proposal which is that he should be paid on an hourly rate until the contract is agreed at which point he will convert that into a percentage of the final build cost. On behalf of the client, the project manager accepts this proposal subject to a capped upper limit. Charles agrees despite the fact that at this stage the contractor and project manager have not finalised the scope of the works and there is no way of telling with precision what the end cost is likely to be. The parties execute a form of appointment incorporating the terms of CE/99.

No alterations are made to the schedule of services although, heeding Desmond's instruction to let the project manager look after money issues and, following some vague discussions to the effect that he should concentrate on design matters, Charles plays little part in contract administration. Although named as the contract administrator in the draft of the contract, Charles allows most of these functions to be undertaken by the project manager.

Two-thirds of the way into the originally envisaged contract period it becomes apparent to all parties that the works are running late. Three other, equally unpalatable conclusions occur separately to the parties. First, the contract manager realises that his original forecasts for the costs of the works will be significantly exceeded. Second, Charles realises that the amount of work done is well in excess of that anticipated, and that he will make a large loss on the job unless he can negotiate additional fees. Third, both Charles and the project manager realise that the lack of co-ordination of the works has led to a clash between the contractor's setting out details and the joinery drawings. A debate occurs as to whether this is the fault of the contractor or Charles for failing to ensure design co-ordination.

Disputes arise. Charles maintains that the scope of works has increased beyond that for which he had originally contracted and Desmond counters by arguing that if this is so (which he contests), it is because Charles was neglectful in his overseeing of the joinery works.[10]

There are two related lessons to be learned here. The first is the danger of agreeing to a fixed or capped fee in circumstances where this is calculated by reference to an uncertain scope of work. The second is the danger of leaving uncertainty as to the circumstances in which additional works may give rise to entitlement to additional payment.

Home-made forms of appointment

So far this chapter has dealt with two extremes – the use of one of the standard forms of appointment, and the use of an unsatisfactory shortcut. This, however, overlooks the large number of appointments where the parties opt to use some form of 'bespoke' appointment produced for the requirements of the particular project. In many cases this will be a form devised by lawyers acting for a particular developer or design and build contractor. Some of these are widely used and, while not becoming standard forms, have acquired recognition in certain parts of the industry as being apt for use on certain types of project. Those who favour the use of such appointments argue that the standard forms are clumsy and require extensive modification to tailor them to the needs of a specific project, and that consequently the use of 'bespoke' drafting allows the needs of a particular job to be addressed with precision.

Particularly where a client seeks to have a number of projects built on substantially similar terms, the advantages are obvious. When used for retail developments or multi-unit housing developments, this approach allows the parties to go forward, confident that they are dealing with a 'tried and tested' appointment, with a resultant possibility of fostering an atmosphere of teamwork.

However, the potential disadvantages are also obvious: such contracts can be, and often are, weighted in favour of the client for whom they have been prepared. Faced with such forms, there is no substitute for seeking appropriate professional advice. It follows from the earlier part of this chapter that the wise architect will resist client pressures to the effect that 'this is the form we always use'. In many cases the architect's scope for negotiating changes will be limited. It is the prerogative of the client to assert that its form is the one it has used before and that the architect can take it or leave it. Faced with this

Getting Paid

ultimatum, architects would be wise to remember that some jobs are best declined. On the positive side, there are an increasing number of instances where developers, particularly those frequently engaged in similar projects, have engaged the same contractors and professionals for subsequent projects on the same or very similar terms. Provided that the terms of the appointment were satisfactory 'first time around' and provided that the projects really do repeat each other, this type of arrangement may work out well for all concerned. For the architect it is important to remember that one of the few things worse than a commercially disastrous project is a succession of commercially disastrous projects. Similarly it is absolutely critical to ensure that any bespoke appointment designed for use in these circumstances is acceptable to insurers.

While each of these forms will be different, most have several common features. The first is the requirement that the architect is to provide collateral warranties, the second is the absence of a clause restricting the client's rights of set-off, and the third the omission of the clauses listed above which protect the architect's right to collect payment.

To the extent that the provision of warranties affects entitlement to payment, this is dealt with at p.45. The question of set-off is addressed in Chapter 5.

Collateral warranties

A collateral warranty is an agreement between a contractor or a sub-contractor or a member of the professional team and a party other than their immediate client. In a traditional contract, architects are frequently required to provide warranties to purchasers, tenants and funders as well as sometimes to other parties such as the owners of reversionary interests in the land, forward funders or adjoining owners affected by the works.

The purpose of the warranty is to create a direct contractual relationship between the architect and the third party such that the third party can seek to sue the architect in the event that the architect fails to perform. The need for warranties grew out of a series of decisions of the courts in the late 1980s in which the courts held that in these circumstances a contractual relationship was required in order for a third party to claim damages. However, direct agreements between members of the construction team collateral to their contract with their client have existed and have been widely used since the early nineteenth century.

SFA/99 clause 7.5: third party agreements provides for the provision of warranties in the BPF Standard Form. Tailor-made forms of appointment almost invariably include a provision requiring the architect to enter into collateral warranties. Usually the appointment will have a draft annexed. Where the architect is engaged by a design and build contractor this will usually be in favour of the employer, and in both traditional and design and build forms, the requirement will usually be to provide warranties in favour of tenants, purchasers and to any bank or other lender providing funding for the development.

It is not unusual to find that the clause requiring the warranty seeks to restrict the architect's right to require amendments, and it is also quite common for the architect's right to stage payments to be made conditional on warranties being completed prior to such payments being made.

Collateral warranties present a problem for architects. They impose additional obligations to a party who is not the architect's client and whose identity is often not ascertained until some time in the future. The architect does not know if this is the sort of person or organisation they would wish to contract with. The terms are usually bespoke and so any sensible architect will show the warranty to both their solicitor and their insurers. The latter is crucial; no warranty is worth the paper it is written on if it is not backed by the architect's insurers (and likely to be by future years' insurers). It is not unknown for insurers to impose conditions for agreeing appointments. While this is never popular with clients, the architect should be careful to remind the client that insurers hold a strong hand; if a condition of continued cover is the agreement of certain terms within the appointment, the client does not have much room for argument. No architect should agree to any draft warranty until they have seen the precise terms. It is quite reasonable for an architect who is presented with a warranty midway through the project to demand additional payment for the

Getting Paid

time and cost of considering it and the additional risk it might impose.

Can a client actually enforce a provision of this sort? Common sense suggests that the answer will be 'yes, subject to some obvious exceptions'. As a general rule, if the warranty has been provided with the architect's appointment and the architect has signed the appointment without demur, it will be difficult to argue that the architect should be excused from signing the warranty.

There are two clear caveats to this. First, the provision requiring the production of warranties must be free from ambiguity. Secondly, any delay in producing the warranties should not be attributable to fault on the part of the client such that the client may be said to be relying on its own breach of the terms of the collateral warranty.

A more difficult question arises if the architect has responded to the draft appointment with annexed warranties with a comment to the effect that while the architect may have no objection in principle, they intend to take the advice of lawyers or insurers. What happens if this is not provided until after the appointment is signed, at which time the architect's advisers raise substantive objections?

There is no clear answer to this issue and it remains to be seen how a court would approach it. It is to be hoped that, in these circumstances, matters would not need to come before a court as the parties would appreciate the uncertainty of their positions and would find an acceptable compromise. In fact, it is also probable that this sort of situation would only arise in unusual circumstances. Insurers are invariably conscious of the need to deal properly and quickly with queries surrounding appointments and warranties.

Endnotes:

1. Strictly speaking this arrangement is probably what is called 'quasi-contract' – the distinction is not important for present purposes.
2. Once again the decision in *Picardi* v *Cuniberti* illustrates the pitfalls awaiting those who do not vigorously attend to finishing these matters.
3. Moxley, R. (1984) *The Architect's Guide to Fee Negotiations*, Architecture and Building Practice Guides Ltd. and Byrom, R.J. (2001) *Terms of Engagement and Fees*, London, RIBA Publications.
4. Even if the client has been involved in the building process, this is no guarantee that he or she will understand, still less agree to the terms of an appointment. Where the client is a private individual this is even more important.
5. Lupton, S. (Ed.) (2002) *Architect's Job Book Seventh Edition*, London, RIBA Enterprises.
6. Tolkein, J. R. R. (1954) 'Shortcuts lead to long delays' *The Lord of the Rings*, London, George Allen and Unwin.
7. A discussion of such exceptions is outside the scope of this book. Generally these exceptions will not be available and will not therefore assist.
8. One interesting argument is that this sort of unequal bargaining power might infringe a party's human rights. Ingenious as this is, the courts are reluctant to give much weight to this in the context of a commercial contract.
9. Readers of the Latham and Egan Reports will doubtless observe that in each there is criticism of an approach to construction which is overly reliant upon contracts at the expense of relationships. Egan goes as far as to commend the approach of the car industry in which many supply agreements function without the need for formal contracts, but this is perhaps to overlook the essential differences between the car and construction industries and the fact that contracts are to supplement not replace relationships.
10. In *Picardi* v *Cuniberti*, although the contract was not signed, there is a lesson which applies to the present situation – the precise scope of the architect's services was left 'in limbo', directly leading to his failure to enforce terms leading to additional payments.

Getting Paid

5 Set-off and counterclaims

Chapter 3 looked at the architect's entitlement to fees. Chapter 4 then considered certain provisions of architect's appointments. Both chapters raised considerations intended to minimise the likelihood of situations such as those described in Chapter 2 occurring.

Disputes do occur and, perhaps unsurprisingly, manifest themselves most often when the architect raises the question of fees, particularly if a large backlog of unpaid fees has been allowed to accumulate. The architect's request for payment is greeted not by a cheque but by a litany of complaints at the performance of the architect. Sometimes this is no great surprise; the relationship between the parties has been deteriorating during the course of the works and the client's complaint simply refines or articulates complaints which have been simmering for some time. In other cases, the complaint comes 'out of a clear blue sky'.

Whatever form the complaints take, they will have two linked consequences. On the one hand it will be said that the architect is not entitled to payment of the sums for which he or she has applied because the services have not been performed properly. On the other it will be alleged that the architect's failures give rise to a claim because the architect's defaults have cost the client money which the client is entitled to claim from the architect. The former is referred to by lawyers as set-off or 'abatement'. The latter is known as a counterclaim. Strictly the term 'set-off' refers only to the former, where matters in complaint are set up as a way to diminish or extinguish the claim. Confusingly, however, the terms are frequently used interchangeably to cover both situations.

In many cases the two are closely linked and can be regarded as two sides of the same coin. However, because they may be treated differently in law, it is necessary to understand the difference between them.

Set-off and counterclaims distinguished

In simple terms, abatement means that certain matters can be taken into account to reduce the sums which would otherwise be due to the architect. Commonly this will occur where the client can establish that particular services forming part of the disputed fee account have not been performed; or where fees only become due if certain milestones are reached, and the relevant event

Getting Paid

has not occurred. In other words, the client argues that the fee account itself can be attacked.

To take a common situation: it is not unusual for fees to become due only when particular work stages have been completed. These may include reaching particular milestones, the most common of which is obtaining planning permission. The precise terms of the architect's entitlement will depend upon the exact nature of the agreement between the parties. However, care is called for: if (for example) planning permission is delayed, perhaps by matters beyond the control of the architect, entitlement to that part of the fees which is dependent upon planning permission may be seriously delayed, and it is no answer to contend that the architect has undertaken a great deal of work and should be paid for what they have done. The architect would be better advised to arrange for fees to become due upon the preparation of a planning application.

The most extreme form of abatement is obviously where the client contends that the works undertaken by the architect have been done badly; so badly in fact that the services performed are valueless. In most instances, this allegation will be followed by the allegation that because of this the client has suffered losses (due for example to the extra cost of having the work done properly) and this gives rise to a counterclaim.

Generally, except where the works done by the architect have been such an unmitigated disaster that they have been utterly useless to the client, this will not be the case and the questions of abatement and counterclaim will arise separately. That is to say, the architect will be entitled to fees in respect of the works properly undertaken, and the client will seek to raise a counterclaim in respect of the works done badly.

It follows that a counterclaim is a claim which arises separately from the fee claim, generally based upon the allegation of professional negligence against the architect. It will be said that the architect performed some or all of the appointment badly, consequent to which the client was obliged to expend additional sums.

Set-off and counterclaims

> **Case Study 4**
>
> Xena has appointed Zack to act as her architect. The appointment issued is a form of SFA/99 in which Schedule 3 was completed to provide for part payment of Zack's fees upon:
>
> - production of outline drawings (10%);
> - part upon completion of detailed design (25%);
> - part upon obtaining planning permission (25%); and
> - the remainder in monthly installments during construction (35%).
>
> The project goes wrong from the start. For various reasons the design is delayed, such that Xena asks for work to begin before completion of the detailed design, and after the depositing of plans with the local authority consent is given for the works to start. Detailed planning permission is never granted.
>
> Zack fails to attend site during the week when the damp proof membrane is installed. He therefore fails to advise that it is punctured in several places by nails.
>
> Damp penetration occurs causing the works to be halted. Remedial works cost thousands of pounds and take weeks to be completed.
>
> Zack is not entitled to his fee stage payments for detailed design and obtaining planning permission. The cost of putting right the damp penetration gives rise to a separate claim.

Probably the most commonly encountered situation is where the architect's fee account would be payable, but for the existence of a counterclaim. The crucial question is whether the client is entitled to set its claim (arising out of the alleged negligence of the architect) against the architect's fee claim. Confusingly, the point is often put by lawyers in these terms: when will the client also be entitled to use its counterclaim by way of abatement or set-off?

Getting Paid

In slightly simpler terms, it will be seen at p.52 that the mere existence of a counterclaim does not automatically entitle the client to set it off against the claim.

The practical consequence of this question will be obvious from a reading of Chapter 2. If the architect can commence proceedings in respect of fees free from the threat of the counterclaim, he or she faces the relatively (in litigation terms) easy task of proving the sum they are entitled to. If on the other hand the architect is compelled not only to prove his or her claim but also to defeat the counterclaim, the task will be exponentially harder, longer and more costly. As mentioned above, one likely outcome is that the architect's insurers will forgo the architect's claimed fees as a condition of any settlement of the negligence claim.

So when can a client set-off its counterclaim? The courts have identified three situations:

- **mutual debts:** where each party owes an identified sum to the other;
- **matters in complaint:** generally speaking this refers to matters of the sort discussed above;
- **equitable set-off:** this is a catch-all expression intended to cover situations where claim and counterclaim are so inextricably linked that it is just and equitable to allow claim and counterclaim to be set off against one another.

In broad terms this will mean that where claim and counterclaim arise out of the same set of events, such as the architect's administration of the contract, the court is likely to permit the counterclaim to be set-off.

This general rule is subject to two limitations:

- restrictions on the right of set-off provided by statute; and
- restrictions imposed by the contract.

Set-off and counterclaims

Restrictions imposed by statute

As a general rule it is unwise to assume that the courts will relieve the architect from the effect of an onerous term. Generally, and as is stressed elsewhere in this book, the terms of an appointment will mean what they say, even if they produce a harsh result for one party.

Limited exceptions are provided by statute. The most significant is the Unfair Contract Terms (UCTA) Act 1977. This limits the right to rely upon exclusion clauses.

The UCTA will apply where one party deals as a consumer or on the other's standard terms of business (an expression which will generally include both standard forms of appointment, and an architect's own form of appointment).

Any provision which seeks to limit or exclude liability in these circumstances will be subject to a test of reasonableness. What is reasonable will depend on the circumstances. A good rule of thumb might be that where the appointment seeks to limit liability to a pre-determined level, perhaps a figure equivalent to an estimate of the construction cost, that may well be held to be reasonable, whereas complete exclusion would not be.[1]

The HGCRA 1996 also serves to restrict rights of set-off.

Section 110 provides that every construction contract subject to the Act shall provide an adequate mechanism for determining what shall be paid and when, and for providing a notice stipulating what would be paid had the parties performed their duties in accordance with the contract; and no set-off is permitted.

Section 111 provides that a party to a construction contract may not withhold payment unless they have served an effective notice of intention to withhold. This must specify the amount proposed to be withheld and the reasons for withholding; and unless otherwise specified must be given no later than seven days prior to the final date when such payment should be made.

Getting Paid

It has been suggested that in the absence of a withholding notice, no set-off is possible. This is probably not the case, and the correct view is probably that the 'receiving party' needs to show that the sums claimed are actually due. If they can do this (i.e. show that they would be due the sums claimed), the absence of a notice under section 111 will almost certainly disqualify the other party from exercising any right of set-off.

Additionally, the parties should be alive to the provisions of section 113. This prohibits the practice of making payment conditional upon receiving payment from another party, except when that other party has become insolvent. This outlaws the often-condemned practice of 'pay when paid' clauses. Where the paying party's client has become insolvent, it may be possible to justify the practice on the basis that 'sharing the blow' might be apt, although even this is difficult in circumstances when the client is better able to absorb such a blow than the architect.

Restrictions imposed by contract

The parties to a contract are at liberty to divide risk in whatever proportion they agree. Risks relating to set-off and counterclaim are no exception. In building contracts they have been common for many years. A good example is provided by the provisions of clause 23 of Dom/1. These provisions, with minimal alteration, was originally found in the Green form of sub-contract for use with JCT63. It sets out a two-stage test:

1. the amount of the set-off has been qualified in detail and with reasonable accuracy;

2. notice has been provided in writing to the sub-contractor no later than 10 days before the sum against which the set-off is to be made should become due.

In the absence of compliance with these two requirements, no set-off can be made. The courts will not hesitate to uphold this and prohibit set-off in such circumstances.

In architects' appointments such provisions are a more recent phenomenon. Examples include clause 5.11 in SFA/99, which excludes rights of set-off except where the parties agree that the sums in question can be set off. The intention of these provisions is clear and is to separate the architect's entitlement to fees from any counterclaim. They do not seek to prevent the client from bringing a claim at all, rather they are intended to ensure that the architect is paid what is due, and if the client wishes in due course to bring a claim, it is entitled to do so.

Endnote:

1 An alternative approach was adopted by the courts in *Moores* v *Yakeley* (1998) 62 Con LR 76, a case involving one of the authors, where the court was happy to see the limit of liability set at a sum equivalent to the estimated sum of the construction works. The UCTA has also been augmented in the case of consumer contracts by a number of sets of regulations. These include the Unfair Terms in Consumer Contracts Regulations 1999, which in turn give effect to the EU Directive on Unfair Terms in Consumer Contracts (OJ 1993 L 95 p.28).

Getting Paid

6 The decision to proceed

The end of the affair

In previous chapters consideration has been given to the circumstances which can lead to disputes over fees. This chapter is concerned with the realisation by the architect that a problem has arisen with the client, and how to proceed. It is also concerned, if only briefly, with steps which might be taken or at least considered in order to prevent the problem developing into a full scale dispute. The starting point is to consider what is meant by a dispute. There have been a number of cases in recent years where one party has commenced proceedings against the other in circumstances where the courts have found that the parties could not properly be said to be in dispute with one another.[1]

Typically it is said in these cases that although one party has asserted an entitlement, the other has either not been given the chance to refute the assertion or has not actually sought to argue.

In the sort of disputes which concern us, this is seldom the case; in fact, the reverse is more likely. Few architects can be accused of jumping the gun and prematurely heading into disputes until they feel they have exhausted every alternative. A frequent concern of many architects (and the issue is dealt with in Chapters 2 and 3) is that they are adopting an excessively contractual position and that this will make their relationship with the client even worse. While many professionals consider, with justification, that to admit that their relationship with the client has broken down is an admission of failure, circumstances can and do arise where such a conclusion has to be reached. Indeed, it is sometimes the case that by struggling on the architect will only make matters worse.

There are obviously no hard and fast rules to govern when the architect should conclude that they are in a dispute with their client. Case Study 5 provides an illustration of the choices which can face the parties. It also lists the tell-tale signs, some or all of which almost always characterise a professional relationship which is in serious decline.

Getting Paid

Case Study 5

Eric is an architect and Fred is the managing director of his client, a small manufacturing business which is having its factory modernised and extended. Prior to these works the business has occupied the premises for a century and none of its staff have experience of building works.

The works include the replacement of fitted cabinets with new made-to-measure joinery. Eric produces drawings using dimensions taken by the contractor. These drawings are supplied to the contractor to use in producing shop drawings. During this process it is discovered that there is an error in the original dimensions which requires Eric to repeat his original drawings which causes the works to be delayed.

While this is happening Fred instructs what he describes as 'minor' variations to the joinery, asserting that these should be capable of being accommodated within the original timeframe, and more worryingly, that they would not have been necessary had the works not suffered from the dimension error. Eric writes warning him that this may 'let the contractor off the hook' in relation to the setting out issues. Fred's response is equivocal but he persists with the request for the variations.

The contractor responds to the instruction for the variation by asserting that this will alter the wall fixings for the cabinets and will also affect delivery times for the cabinets due to the need to source and obtain materials. An extension of time is sought. Eric informs Fred, who does not respond.

Eric takes the opportunity to write to Fred seeking additional fees for the re-drawing exercise. Fred does not respond. A few weeks later Eric sends a reminder and is met with a letter from the company's solicitors alleging that the whole problem has arisen from Eric's failure properly to oversee the contractor and to check the accuracy of the dimensions.

The decision to proceed

> **'The Rake's Progress'**
> - Increasing difficulty in obtaining clear instructions.
> - Delay in securing payment of fee accounts.
> - Increasingly strained interpersonal relations with employer – architect's judgement called into question.
> - Disagreements over instructions, particularly whether certain matters constitute variations.
> - Debates over progress and the architect's perceived failure to procure adherence to programme dates.
> - Legal advice sought by employer.

From the architect's perspective, the works will be overshadowed by a sense that his or her authority is being undermined and the ability to successfully run the project. No doubt this is matched by a feeling on the part of the client that the project is running out of control and that it is not being effectively managed and hence its interests are not being protected. Figure 2 takes the matters described in Case Study 5 and considers them from the perspectives of the client and the architect. It is worth reflecting that on the same facts, the differing perspectives of the parties mean that each can quite genuinely form diametrically opposed views.

It might be suggested that the client's reaction is typical of someone anxious to find fault and locate a reason not to pay for professional services. However, to adopt this view is largely to miss the point. It may well be that the client has failed to understand that the need for a variation is actually a result of its own conduct. Similarly it may be that the client has misunderstood the timing consequences of particular events, perhaps attaching undue weight to a matter which will actually not cause delay to the project. To see ourselves as others see us is a gift not given to many.

Looking again at Case Study 5, the main point is this: the problems which occur are all capable of resolution. However, the architect does not address the issues and consequently the problems are allowed to grow. In this respect at least, the architect in Case Study 5 is culpable: the architect is the professional and it is down to him or her to ensure that the client understands the effect and consequences of particular issues such that it can form a considered judgement.

Issue	Client's perspective	Architect's perspective
Setting out difficulty following error in contractor's shop drawings requiring re-execution of architect's drawings.	The architect has permitted this error to arise as a result of inadequate attention to detail.	The contractor's carelessness was not something within the architect's control and this has necessitated additional work for which payment is due.
The resultant delays.	These would not have occurred but for the original error by the architect or the contractor; which of them is unimportant, it was for the architect to ensure that such things did not happen.	This is the fault of the contractor for which no extension is due.
Possible further delays resulting from the client's variations.	These are not really variations at all: but for the setting out mistake these could have been accommodated within the original design.	This will cause delay and may have the effect of relieving the contractor from the consequence of the setting out error.

Figure 2: A dispute from the perspectives of client and architect

The decision to proceed

What should be done?

Faced with the deteriorating situation described in Case Study 5 and summarised in Figure 2, all but the most incurably naive optimist would accept that a dispute between the parties was imminent and probably inevitable. Of the various options open to the architect, probably the least advisable is to attempt to carry on as if nothing was wrong.

In this sort of situation some of the most frequently asked questions will include the following:

Q: Is it worth attempting to confront the client and bring matters to a head?
A: Certainly. The worst that will happen will be that all of the client's complaints will come to the surface, and the dispute may be brought forward. It is sensible to remember in these circumstances that the parties' actions may well be scrutinised at some later date by a court or arbitrator, and therefore an appearance of reasonableness is to be encouraged. The approach which is often adopted here is to suggest that while there are some important issues which need to be resolved, these issues will not prevent the project being built, and that common sense suggests that the parties should attempt to put these to one side until the job is complete. Pragmatic as this suggestion is, it will not work where confidence and trust have broken down.

Q: Can work be suspended or cease altogether?
A: This is both a legal and a tactical question. Where the contract between the parties is subject to the provisions of the HGCRA 1996, section 112 provides a right to suspend where a sum due is not paid by the final date for payment and no valid withholding notice has been given,[2] provided that at least seven days notice has been given. It is important to remember that this will not apply to domestic works. Where it does apply it is important first to observe strictly the notice provisions, and second to consider whether suspension will provide the parties with a cooling off period in which they can reflect upon and hopefully narrow their differences or whether this will be the last straw which precipitates them into a dispute.

Getting Paid

Where the Act does not apply the parties will be regulated by the terms of the appointment. SFA/99 summarised below, provides by clause 8.2 that:

> in the event of the client being in default of payment of any of our fees or other amounts due the Architect may suspend his obligations on giving at least 7 days notice of the intention to suspend his obligations and stating the grounds for doing so and the obligations affected. The Architect shall resume performance of his obligations on receipt of the outstanding amounts.

It is also worth noting that clause 5.13 provides for the payment of interest on late settlements of monies.

In the event that the appointment does not contain detailed provisions for determination or suspension, the parties' rights are governed by the common law. As set out above the great majority of contracts for architectural services are 'entire contracts' which means that the architect is obliged to provide all of the services which they are contracted for.

In practice this means that the right to suspend or determine performance is limited. As a general rule, unless it can be shown that there is what is called a 'repudiatory breach', the architect will not be entitled to determine. Figure 3 sets out some circumstances in which the architect will generally be entitled to terminate his appointment. In legal terms, however, the test is whether one party can be shown to have conducted themselves in a way which shows an intention no longer to be bound by the terms of the contract.

Repudiatory breach
- Insolvency of client.
- Persistent interference with architect's role.
- Persistent non-payment.
- Where provided by the appointment, suspension for longer than the specified period.

Figure 3: Repudiatory breach

The decision to proceed

It will be obvious that this is not something to be done lightly. Where one party wrongly terminates a contract they will be faced with a claim for damages; where the architect wrongly treats the contract as being repudiated they face a claim for the additional cost of employing another architect. The moral therefore is that this is a step only to be taken in extreme circumstances. It is entirely conceivable that if an architect is not protected by a clause allowing suspension of services for non-payment such as those included in SFA/99 and CE/99, the architect may be required to continue working when there may be no hope of further payment.

Q: Should insurers be notified?
A: Almost certainly. Although there may well be no indication that a claim of professional negligence will be made, it is easy to see from Case Study 5 that this is often only a short step away. On the one hand, this demonstrates to insurers a responsible attitude, and on the other, it improves the likelihood of insurers being amenable to the insured pursuing a claim for fees. Indeed the view taken by one leading underwriter of architect's professional indemnity insurance can be summed up as follows:

- a dispute over fees will be regarded as an event warranting notification, and
- except where there are compelling contrary reasons, such claims should be aired sooner rather than later; because
- in their experience, where such fee claims are left until late in the project or even after completion they are more likely to develop into claims requiring the involvement of insurers.

Of course, this requires a measure of objectivity on the part of the architect. If the real reason for the non-payment of fees is a genuine failure to perform on the part of the architect, there is very little point in pressing a claim for fees, since this will inevitably be met by a substantial counterclaim, and the net result will be payment by insurers – who are to be forgiven if they are keen to discourage fee claims in these circumstances.

Choice of Forum

Method	Pros	Cons
Insolvency (i.e. winding up or bankruptcy)	■ Relatively quick ■ Effective in clear cases	■ Inappropriate where entitlement disputed ■ Can backfire where actually insolvent
Adjudication	■ Quick ■ Cheap ■ Informal	■ Increasing procedural complexity ■ Informality of procedures produces uncertain results ■ Not generally available for works to private dwellings
Mediation	■ Quick ■ Cheap ■ Consensual	■ Only effective if parties want it to work ■ Dependent on skill of mediator
Arbitration	■ Flexible procedure ■ Perceived as decision involving 'technical matters for technical men'	■ Can be slow and expensive ■ Dependent on skill of an arbitrator
Litigation	■ Formal regulated procedure ■ Commands respect	■ Still slow ■ Can be inflexible

Figure 4: Choice of forum

The decision to proceed

Q: Once a threat of litigation is made, can it be withdrawn?
A: There is a widely held misconception that once a dispute 'goes legal' a process is put in motion which is out of the hands of the parties. This is not the case. The nineteenth century political thinker Clausewitz said that 'War is simply diplomacy carried out by other means'. By the same token, litigation is no more than negotiation by other means. No doubt the decision to commence proceedings is a difficult one emotionally, but it is this which makes the decision seem momentous. The mere act of commencing proceedings is not to be regarded as some irreversible commitment.

Choice of proceedings

Having reached the decision to pursue a fee claim the architect will find a potentially bewildering choice of procedures are available. The choice will be dictated to a large degree by the nature of the dispute. Figure 4 sets out some of the pros and cons, which are then discussed in more detail at p.66.

Insolvency procedures

This covers two situations. Where the client is an individual, the ultimate aim is a bankruptcy order against that individual. Where the client is a limited company the ultimate aim is a winding up order against the company. The procedural steps are broadly the same for both. It should be noted that the procedures are only available where the sum claimed exceeds £750.

The procedure is intended to cover circumstances where the company or individual ('the debtor') is unable to pay their debts as they fall due. The person pursuing the debt ('the creditor') will therefore ask the court to make an order for the winding up or bankruptcy, as the case may be, of the debtor.

As a general observation, the insolvency procedures are a useful threat in certain circumstances. That usefulness is limited to circumstances where there is really no reason for non-payment. Otherwise, while this procedure is superficially attractive – after all the ultimate sanction is about as serious as it gets – it can be a very blunt instrument.

There are two linked reasons for this. Understandably, the courts are loathe to make a winding up or bankruptcy order lightly, and will not do so where there is a reasonable measure of doubt as to whether the debt is due.[3] Additionally, it is likely that, in most instances, the last thing the creditor actually wants is for the debtor to be wound up or declared bankrupt since in this event the chances of obtaining payment will probably disappear altogether.

In short, this is a procedure which is probably less attractive than it appears at first sight.

Adjudication

Where the contract in question is covered by the HGCRA 1996,[4] section 108 provides a right to have disputes or differences dealt with by adjudication. Adjudication is addressed in other contexts elsewhere.[5] The obvious attraction of adjudication is that it is a quick and efficient means of allowing disputes to be determined. Except in exceptional circumstances, an adjudication will take no more than 28 days (or 42 if the referring party (the claimant) requests) and the adjudicator's decision will be binding unless or until reversed by agreement or by subsequent litigation or arbitration. The obvious shortcoming (considered in some detail in Chapter 8) is that adjudication is not available in most disputes arising out of works to private dwellings.

Accordingly, adjudication can be and often is an ideal way of achieving a quick and effective solution to disputes. On the negative side, adjudication is criticised because the need to produce quick decisions can lead to unsatisfactory results; sometimes because the time constraints have meant that issues have been inadequately investigated; in other cases the courts have declined to enforce decisions which have been reached where the parties have (usually because they have been acting under time constraints) offended against either rules governing adjudication procedure, or more fundamental considerations of natural justice.[6] These issues are considered further in Chapter 8.

The speed and informality of adjudications has been a cause of concern among insurers who have regarded adjudication as likely to produce uncertain

The decision to proceed

and inconsistent results. Contrary to certain suggestions, this does not result from a wish to 'put off the evil hour'; rather it is because the insurance industry is dependent upon the ability to assess risk, and thus to set reserves. Where this certainty is lacking, insurers will be understandably apprehensive. To an extent this view is softening with the increased prevalence of adjudication. However it remains understandably an anxiety.

A more pragmatic concern is the fact that, except where the parties use SFA/99 and CE/95 or amend the relevant contract conditions, there is no entitlement to costs. Hence there is a risk where relatively modest sums are involved that a significant proportion of the sum at stake will be absorbed in costs.

Mediation

Mediation is the process whereby the parties agree to appoint a neutral third party who seeks to facilitate and broker a settlement. Mediation is different from any other means of dispute resolution because it does not involve any decision as to the merits of the parties' respective contentions. It tends to comprise the exchange by the parties of brief position statements summarising their respective positions, followed by a meeting which will typically commence with a brief plenary session at which the parties make short opening statements followed by a series of caucuses at which the mediator will see each party individually, revealing to the other only what he or she has been authorised to divulge. By this process it is hoped that a settlement can be achieved, and unquestionably the process has been and is becoming increasingly successful.[7]

That success has generally been achieved in cases where the parties want to settle their differences and believe that through sensible negotiation this can be achieved. Where one party adamantly maintains, for example, that there is nothing to pay and no way in which they are going to budge, the likelihood of success diminishes.

By contrast with adjudication, mediation has been popular with insurers. The reasons arise from similar issues to the concerns over adjudication: the mediation process enables insurers to keep a measure of control over

Getting Paid

the result, and it is widely perceived that the mediation process is helpful in managing the expectations of opposing parties.

Arbitration

All of the standard forms of architect's appointments contain provisions for disputes to be referred to arbitration. Arbitration procedure is set out in more detail in Chapter 7. In the great majority of cases the parties will either agree to the appointment of a particular individual or will agree to an arbitrator being nominated by the body named in the appointment. The arbitrator sets down a procedural timetable which will generally involve the service of 'statements of case' in which the parties set out their respective contentions together with relevant supporting documents; followed by (where appropriate) provision for inspection of any further relevant documents, exchange of witnesses and experts' reports. In simple cases the arbitrator can direct that the matter will be dealt with on a 'documents only' basis without the need for a formal hearing. In more complex cases they will usually direct that there should be a hearing at which witnesses can be called and cross-examined.

The most frequently cited criticism of arbitration is that it is slow and expensive. Although the procedure for dealing with arbitration has been significantly improved following the enactment of the Arbitration Act 1996, it is still not unusual for relatively simple matters to take over a year to be dealt with. In addition to their own costs the parties will also be liable for the costs of the arbitrator. Furthermore, while opinions are divided, misgivings are frequently voiced as to the efficacy of arbitration as a means of dealing with disputes, and as to the quality of some arbitrators.[8]

It is, however, the case that while arbitration is not the ideal means to resolve disputes over fees, it is the most commonly used procedure in instances where adjudication is not available.[9]

Litigation

Where adjudication is not available and where the appointment does not contain provision for arbitration the parties will be compelled to litigate. Since 1998, court procedures have undergone a radical overhaul under the 'Woolf

The decision to proceed

Reforms', named after Lord Woolf, the Master of the Rolls, the senior judge in the Court of Appeal.

The stated intention of the Woolf Reforms is to simplify the litigation process, and to introduce procedural rules which allow disputes to be dealt with in a way which is proportionate to the sums at stake and the complexity of the issues.

Applied to most disputes over fees, which will generally involve modest sums of money and relatively straightforward facts, the most important innovation has been the introduction of the 'fast track', the purpose of which is to enable smaller claims to be dealt with in a streamlined form with the intention that such matters should be capable of being disposed of in a maximum of six months. Although the reforms have encountered (and are continuing to experience) some significant teething troubles, it is likely that court proceedings will become an increasingly appropriate and attractive method of resolving fee disputes.

Endnotes:

1. Typically this has arisen in the context of adjudication. An adjudication cannot be brought unless there is a dispute, and the courts have not hesitated to conclude that in some cases the parties have commenced an adjudication before it could be said that a dispute existed. Generally, for a dispute to exist party A asserts an entitlement, party B disputes that entitlement and party A reasserts that entitlement. This matter is usefully discussed by Thornton HHJ QC in *Fast Track* v *Morrison* (2000) 75 Con LR 33.

2. See Chapter 5 on set-off and Chapter 8 on adjudication.

3. The Companies Court has frequently indicated that the winding up and bankruptcy procedure is not to be used as a method of debt collection where there is a dispute over the debt. Self-evidently, the debtor will defeat the winding up or bankruptcy petition where they can show there is a genuine dispute over the sum claimed.

4. i.e. it is concerned with a contract which came into being after 31 May 1998 and it is not concerned with works to a dwelling. (While there are other exceptions to the application of the Act, they generally fall outside the scope of this book.)

5. See in particular Chapter 8 regarding the adjudication procedure.

6. It is worth considering the decision of HHJ Bowsher QC in *Discain* v *Opecprime Developments Ltd* [2000] BLR 402 which is a salutary lesson in how easy it is to cross the line between what is expedient in order to move a matter forward and what may run the risk of appearing unfair and unjust.

7 Mediation has been imported into the United Kingdom in the course of the last decade from the United States where it was developed during the 1970s and 1980s to deal with large class actions. One of the principals in the development of mediation, David Shapiro, is now practising in London and is a consultant to a leading law firm.

8 This is not a view held by the authors although they acknowledge that arbitration procedure can sometimes go awry.

9 See Chapter 7.

7 Litigation and arbitration

Introduction

The expression 'taking someone to court' and its reverse side 'being taken to court', like many phrases which sell newspapers, is both colourful and misleading in equal measures.

While conjuring up an image of uniformed tipstaffs appearing to escort the hapless defendant to some imposing gothic testament to the legal system, it also suggests that this is an immediate process and that not only do the parties find themselves whisked at little notice before the court but that once started the legal process cranks over into some sort of inexorable machine which the parties have little power to control or influence.

Confusingly, and with few attempts at explanation, journalists also occasionally delight in stories of disputes which have creaked along for years in the style of Charles Dickens's *Bleak House*.

Arbitration does not get a better press. To the extent that it receives any coverage at all, it tends to be regarded as a shadowy process taking place behind closed doors amid an atmosphere of some mystery.

As a consequence, formal legal proceedings, whether in arbitration or litigation, are widely treated with mistrust and misunderstanding. There is a general view that they are inaccessible and unintelligible and that to the extent that a result is ever obtained it is a kind of lottery win achieved following the lengthy and ruinously costly exchange by lawyers of incomprehensible jargon from which the majority of laymen are wholly excluded.

Like all myths, those highlighted above have some basis in fact. However, to a large extent they are out of date and exaggerated. In the present day, most forms of proceedings – at least those with which we are concerned – whether in litigation or arbitration, take place in a setting which is geared towards the efficient disposal of commercial disputes and take a form and use language which is reasonably understandable by most people. Some clients unreasonably withhold payment purely in the hope that the architect will not have the determination to pursue them for the sums due. The architect should

Getting Paid

always do everything to disabuse them of this. Once it has become clear that a client is not going to pay, it is usually best to put the matter in the hands of the architect's solicitors. A letter and threat action from them implies resolve and can sometimes work wonders. There can be a further advantage in doing this. Usually a solicitor's letter threatening action will induce the client to engage its own solicitor. The client will then have the benefit (hopefully) of clear advice unclouded by the anger that often builds up in these situations. This can pave the way to settlement. The architect should never indicate how much the non-payment is hurting, perhaps in an attempt to win the client's sympathy – it will usually have the effect of encouraging the non-payment.

The main reasons why many architects have previously not been willing to contemplate taking proceedings are the burden of funding the action and the risk of having to pay security for costs. Approaches for avoiding these problems have been set out above: invoicing frequently for relatively small amounts and ensuring that a provision such as clause 9.5.3 of SFA/99 prohibiting security for costs is included in the architect–client agreement. While the architect will often have to fund his or her side of the action until its conclusion, they can take comfort in SFA/99 clause 9.6 which provides that the architect will be almost wholly reimbursed for their legal costs, and most importantly, also for their own time in conducting the action if they win. Moreover, if an architect can find lawyers prepared to take instructions on a conditional fee agreement (CFA) basis, this can to a very great extent mitigate this problem.

The provisions of SFA/99, introduced only in 1999 and 2000, serve as a very useful deterrent against any client who is tempted to withhold fees unreasonably. Not only does the client risk losing any action and having to pay the fees due, it also risks having to pay the full legal costs of both sides and the architect's costs as well. Once this is explained to the client (hence the importance of getting good legal advice), the architect may find that the client is more likely to be amenable to a reasonable settlement.

Litigation and arbitration

However, although 95 per cent of actions are settled before reaching court, some clients are so convinced of the merits of their cases that they persist in non-payment and the architect is left with no option but to proceed with an action if they are to have any hope of obtaining payment.

The costs of a legal action can be substantial. Solicitors generally charge considerably more per hour than do architects; barristers even more. It is essential, as noted in Chapter 2, that the architect's job file is in perfect order and sets out all the details of the case in a clear and unambiguous fashion that can be quickly understood by a third party unfamiliar with the details of the case. It is usually an advantage to employ a solicitor who specialises in building contract law who will have some understanding of the building industry. The architect should take a keen interest in the progress of the case to ensure that the legal team fully understand the case history as it progresses. However, as solicitors generally charge for each six minutes spent on every case, every discussion will add to the legal costs. It is hoped that any general questions that the architect might have, for example, about legal procedure, will be answered by this book.

The purpose of this chapter is not to attempt to provide a comprehensive explanation of how civil procedure operates,[1] but to provide a reasonably brief guide to the steps which are to be taken in a process of litigation or arbitration. Figures 5 and 6 set out in flowchart form the procedural steps involved in arbitration and litigation which are discussed in the remainder of this chapter. There is also a glossary of expressions commonly used in each in Appendix 3.

Getting Paid

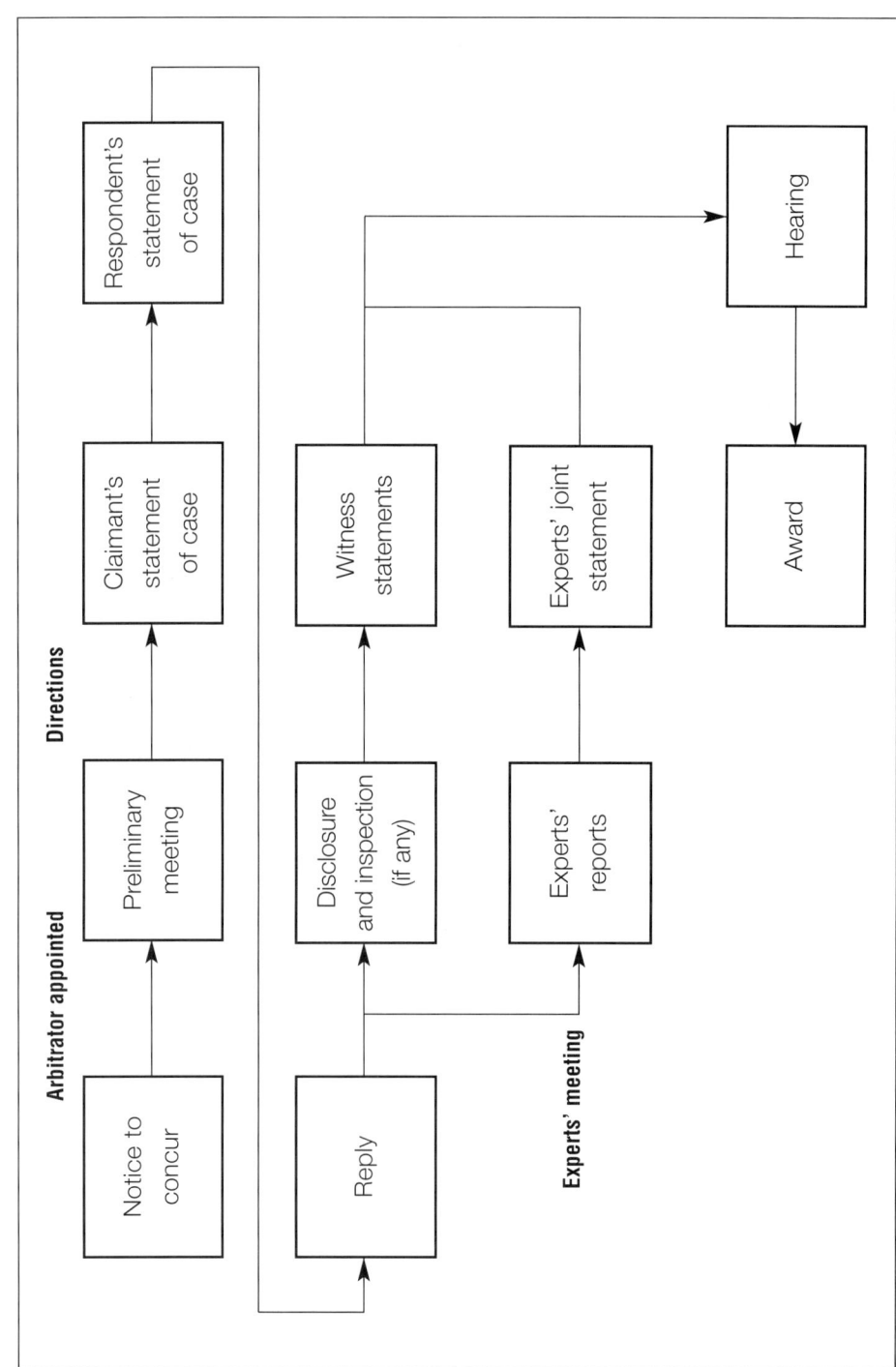

Figure 5: Steps in arbitration

Litigation and arbitration

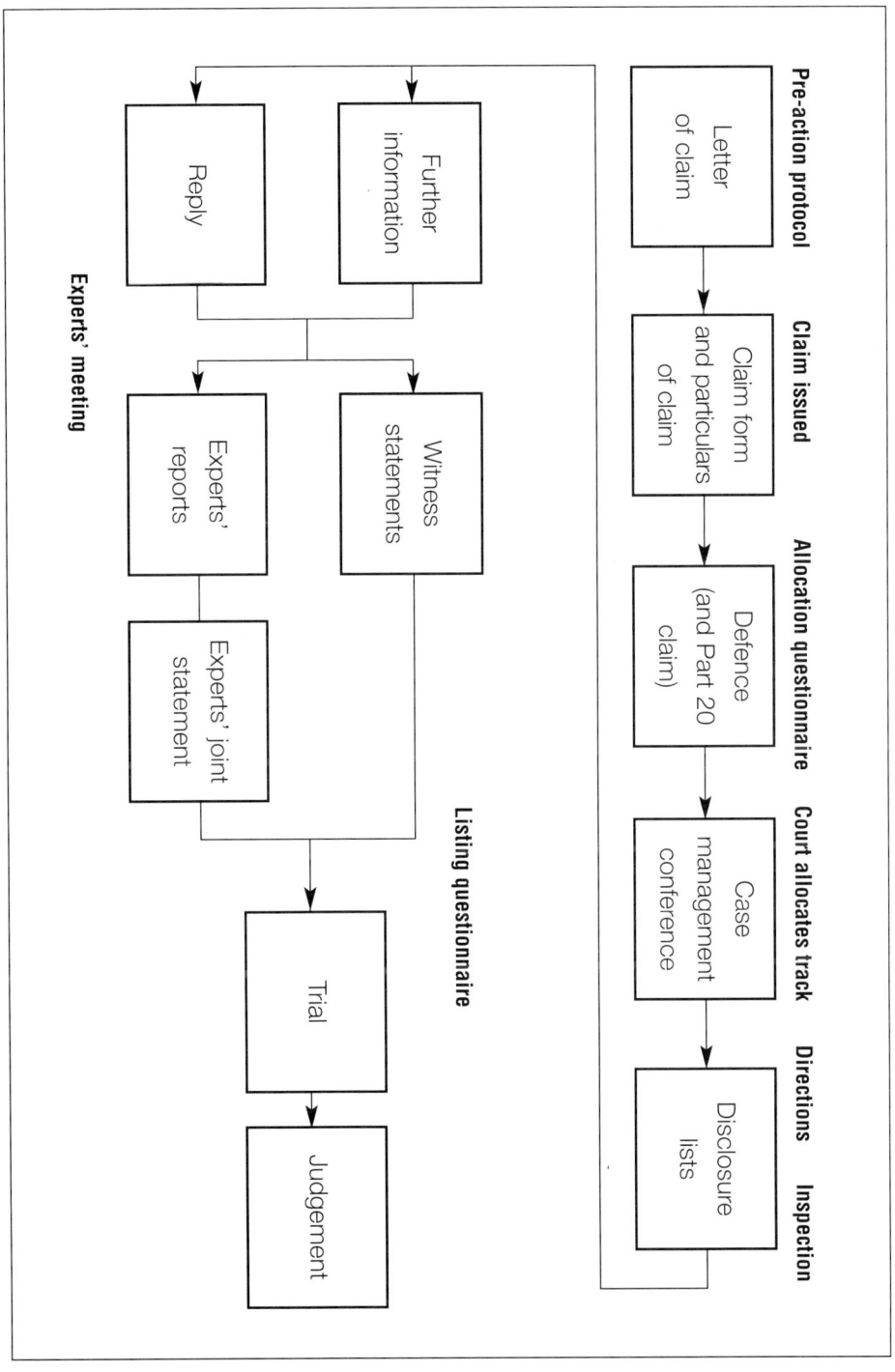

Figure 6: Steps in litigation

Litigation or arbitration: which to choose?

Most standard forms of appointment (including SFA/99) contain an arbitration clause which provides that the parties will refer their differences to arbitration. Commonly, however, where the appointment is a tailor-made document or where the contract is concluded by an exchange of letters, it will not. It is of course open to the parties to reach an ad hoc arrangement to appoint an arbitrator in these circumstances should they consider it appropriate, but more usually the parties will resolve their differences through the courts.

Where the appointment contains an arbitration clause, generally the parties will be constrained to go to arbitration. Indeed, if in these circumstances one party commences proceedings in court the other can apply to the court to have the action 'stayed' to arbitration which means that the action is placed on an indefinite hold while the parties pursue their differences through arbitration.

In other words, in many instances the choice of forum is effectively made for the parties – as a matter of public policy parties are encouraged to use arbitration where available.

Is one to be preferred over the other? Figure 7 sets out some considerations.

The conclusion is that there is not much to choose between arbitration and litigation; the fact that circumstances dictate one rather than the other should not be a cause for concern. In the case of claims for fees, most lawyers will express a preference for the courts, arguing that the courts are generally inclined to take a more robust approach, particularly when faced by reasons for non-payment which appear shadowy or insubstantial.

Privacy	Arbitration is private, but this is seldom a real concern except in high profile matters
Formality	Arbitration is often thought to be less formal, but since the Woolf reforms the reverse is sometimes true
Flexibility	Arbitration procedure is more flexible
Experience	Lay arbitrators have experience of industry conditions: the key consideration is the extent of the arbitrator's skill as an arbitrator rather than perceived industry familiarity
Cost	There is little to choose between them although parties will need to pay for an arbitrator
Security for costs	Arbitrators can be bound by the parties not to grant an order for security for costs (for example, SFA/99 clause 9.5.3) while the courts cannot
Speed	The courts are now often quicker
Quality of decision-making	This is entirely dependent upon the individual tribunal
Summary procedure	This is available in both, but is generally easier to obtain in litigation

Figure 7: Arbitration versus litigation

Overriding objectives and protocols

In the late 1980s and early 1990s both arbitration and litigation underwent detailed scrutiny leading to major procedural reform.[2] For arbitration this took the form of the Arbitration Act 1996, for litigation, of the Civil Procedure Rules (CPR).

While different in many respects, the resulting procedural codes have much in common. In particular both start with a statement of intent. Part 1 of the Civil Procedure Rules[3] comprises the 'overriding objective':

1.1 (1) These rules are a new procedural code with the overriding objective of enabling the court to deal with cases justly.
(2) Dealing with a case justly includes, so far as is practicable:
   (a) ensuring that the parties are on an equal footing;
   (b) saving expense;
   (c) dealing with the case in ways which are proportionate:
      (i) to the amount of money involved;
      (ii) to the importance of the case;
      (iii) to the complexity of the issues; and
      (iv) to the financial position of each party;

   (d) ensuring that it is dealt with expeditiously;
   (e) allotting to it an appropriate share of the court's resources, while taking into account the need to allot resources to other cases.

Application by the court of the overriding objective
1.2 The court must seek to give effect to the overriding objective when it:
   (a) exercises any power given to it by the Rules; or
   (b) interprets any rule.

Duty of the parties
1.3 The parties are required to help the court to further the overriding objective.

Section 1(a) of the Arbitration Act is expressed in similar terms:

> The object of arbitration is to obtain the fair resolution of disputes by an impartial tribunal without unnecessary delay or expense.

The inference to be drawn is that both are to be regarded as a means of resolving disputes in an appropriate manner, rather than as providing a forum for gladiatorial contest. The court is given extensive case management powers in order to compel compliance by the parties with the overriding objective, and these include the power to penalise the parties in terms of costs orders and orders which stay (that is to say freeze) the proceedings, or even by way of requiring one party to pay a sum of money into the court's bank account in the event of failure to comply with any procedural rule.

This theme is also encountered in the Pre-Action Protocol for the Construction and Engineering Disputes[4] to which the great majority of the disputes with which we are concerned will be subject.[5] The purpose of the Protocol is to set out various steps which should be taken by the parties prior to the commencement of proceedings in an attempt to encourage the early exchange of information, to enable the parties to avoid litigation by encouraging settlement and by supporting the efficient management of proceedings where litigation cannot be avoided.

The principal provisions of the Protocol are as follows:

General Aim

2   The general aim of this Protocol is to ensure that before court proceedings commence:

   (i) the claimant and the defendant have provided sufficient information for each party to know the nature of the other's case;
   (ii) each party has had an opportunity to consider the other's case, and to accept or reject all or part of the case made against him at the earliest possible stage;
   (iii) there is more pre-action contact between the parties;

Getting Paid

(iv) better and earlier exchange of information occurs;
(v) there is better pre-action investigations by the parties;
(vi) the parties have met formally on at least one occasion with a view to:

- defining and agreeing the issues between them; and
- exploring possible ways by which the claim may be resolved;

(vii) the parties are in a position where they may be able to settle cases early and fairly without recourse to litigation; and
(viii) proceedings will be conducted efficiently if litigation does become necessary.

Letter of Claim

3   Prior to commencing proceedings, the claimant or his solicitor shall send to each proposed defendant (if appropriate to his registered address) a copy of a letter of claim which shall contain the following:

(i) the claimant's full name and address;
(ii) the full name and address of each proposed defendant;
(iii) a clear summary of the facts on which each claim is based;
(iv) the basis on which each claim is made, identifying the principal contractual terms and statutory provisions relied on;
(v) the nature of the relief claimed; if damages are claimed, a breakdown showing how the damages have been quantified; if a sum is claimed pursuant to a contract, what that sum is;
(vi) if the claimant's claim has been submitted and rejected and the claimant is able to identify the reason(s) for such rejection, the claimant's grounds of belief as to why the claim was wrongly rejected;
(vii) the names of any experts already instructed by the claimant on whose evidence he intends to rely, identifying the issues to which that evidence will be directed.

4. Defendant's Response

The Defendant's acknowledgement

4.1 Within 14 calendar days of receipt of the letter of claim, the defendant should acknowledge its receipt in writing and may give the name and address of his insurer (if any). If there has been no acknowledgement by or on behalf of the defendant within 14 days, the claimant will be entitled to commence proceedings without further compliance with this Protocol.

Objections to the Court's Jurisdiction or the named Defendant

4.2.1 If the Defendant intends to take any objection to all or any part of the claimant's claim on the grounds that (i) the court lacks jurisdiction, (ii) the matter should be referred to arbitration, or (iii) the defendant named in the letter of claim is the wrong defendant within 28 days after receipt of the letter of claim. The letter lists the grounds relied on, and, where appropriate, shall identify the correct defendant (if known). Any failure to take such objection shall not prejudice the defendant's rights to do so in any subsequent proceedings, but the court may take such failure into account when considering the question of costs.

4.2.2 Where such notice of objection is given, the defendant is not required to send a letter of response in accordance with paragraph 4.3.1 in relation to the claim or those parts of it to which the objection relates (as the case may be).

4.2.3 If at any stage before the claimant commences proceedings, the defendant withdraws his objections, then paragraph 4.3 and the remaining part of this Protocol will apply to the claim or those parts of it to which the objection related as if the letter of claim had been received on the date on which notice of withdrawal of the objection had been given.

Getting Paid

The Defendant's response

4.3

4.3.1 Within 28 days from the date of receipt of the letter of claim, or such other period as the parties may reasonably agree (up to a maximum of 4 months), the defendant shall send a letter of response to the claimant which shall contain the following information:

(i) the facts set out in the letter of claim which are agreed or not agreed, and if not agreed, the basis of the disagreement;

(ii) which claims are accepted and which are rejected, and if rejected, the basis of rejection;

(iii) if a claim is accepted in whole or in part, whether the damages, sums or extensions of time claimed are accepted or rejected, and if rejected, the basis of the rejection;

(iv) if contributory negligence is alleged against the claimant, a summary of the facts relied on;

(v) whether the defendant intends to make a counterclaim, and if so, giving the information which is required to be given in a letter of claim by paragraph 3(iii) to (vi) above;

(vi) the names of any experts already instructed on whose evidence it is intended to rely, identifying the issues to which that evidence will be directed.

4.3.2 If no such response is received by the claimant within the period of 28 days (or such other period as has been agreed between the parties), the claimant shall be entitled to commence proceedings without further compliance with this Protocol.

Claimant's response to counterclaim

4.4 The claimant shall provide a response to any counterclaim within the equivalent period allowed to the defendant to respond to the letter of claim under paragraph 4.3.1 above.

5. Pre-Action Meeting

5.1 As soon as possible after receipt by the claimant of the defendant's letter of response, or (if the claimant intends to respond to the counterclaim) after receipt by the defendant of the claimant's letter of response to the counterclaim, the parties should normally meet.

5.2 The aim of the meeting is for the parties to agree what are the main issues in the case, to identify the root cause of disagreement in respect of each issue, and to consider (i) whether, and if so how, the issues might be resolved without recourse to litigation, and (ii) if litigation is unavoidable, what steps should be taken to ensure that it is conducted in accordance with the overriding objective as defined in Part 1.1 of the Civil Practice Rules.

5.3 In some circumstances, it may be necessary to convene more than one meeting. It is not intended by this Protocol to prescribe in detail the manner in which the meetings should be conducted. But the court will normally expect that those attending will include:

(i) where the party is an individual, that individual, and where the party is a corporate body, a representative of that body who has authority to settle the dispute;
(ii) a legal representative of each party (if one has been instructed);
(iii) where the involvement of insurers has been disclosed, a representative of the insurer (who may be its legal representative); and
(iv) where a claim is made or defended on behalf of some other party (such as, for example, a claim made by a main contractor pursuant to a contractual obligation to pass on subcontractor claims), the party on whose behalf the claim is made or defended and/or his legal representatives.

5.4 In respect of each agreed issue or the dispute as a whole, the parties should consider whether some form of alternative dispute resolution procedure would be more suitable than litigation, and if so, endeavour to agree which form to adopt.

Getting Paid

5.5 If the parties are unable to agree on a means of resolving the dispute other than by litigation they should use their best endeavours to agree:
  (i) whether, if there is any area where expert evidence is likely to be required, a joint expert may be appointed, and if so, who that should be; and (so far as is practicable)
  (ii) the extent of disclosure of documents with a view to saving costs; and
  (iii) the conduct of the litigation with the aim of minimising costs and delay.

5.6 Any party who attended any pre-action meeting shall be at liberty to disclose to the court:
  (i) that the meeting took place, when and who attended;
  (ii) the identity of any party who refused to attend, and the grounds for such refusal;
  (iii) if the meeting did not take place, why not; and
  (iv) any agreements concluded between the parties.

5.7 Except as provided in paragraph 5.6, everything said at pre-action meeting shall be treated as 'without prejudice'.

In the context of fee claims these provisions are highly significant. It is incumbent upon the parties to put their 'cards on the table' and to set out the detail of their respective claims. It is no longer possible for a party to rely upon a bare denial that the other is entitled to the sums claimed. There is a positive duty on the parties to approach the matter in a way which encourages settlement.

The exchange of letters of claim and the response to the letter of claim, and the requirement for a pre-action meeting provide the parties with the opportunity to consider whether their case is as strong as they may believe. At the very least, where a client has expressed reasons for non-payment which emanate from the breakdown of relations with the architect, it is an opportunity to examine whether those really are matters which provide a reason for non-payment.

No comparable provisions exist under the Arbitration Act 1996. It is of course open to the claimant to suggest to the defendant that the provisions of the Protocol should be adopted, but there is no obligation on the respondent to agree to this save that, as discussed at p.105, the arbitrator has a discretion to take such matters into account in making the costs order.

It will be appreciated that in the sort of claims with which this book is concerned, the claimant will frequently be pursuing relatively small sums and that in most cases it is to the advantage of the claimant to argue that the matter raises none of the complexities which would justify proceedings in the High Court.

Litigation procedure

Starting proceedings

Proceedings are formally commenced by a claimant completing a claim form which is then issued by a court office who date it and stamp it with the court seal. An example is in Appendix 4.[6]

For the type of claims with which we are concerned, where the sum at stake is below £15,000, the claimant must issue the claim in the county court. Otherwise, the claimant has a choice whether to issue in the High Court or the county court. The decision is usually based upon the factors set out in Figure 8. With architect's fee claims, where proceedings are issued in the High Court, they should be issued in the Technology and Construction Court[7] which is the branch of the High Court that, as the name suggests, deals with construction cases.

Getting Paid

Nature of claim	Where to issue
Under £15,000	must be county court
Large sums at stake	High Court preferable
Complex questions of fact	High Court preferable
Detailed technical evidence	High Court preferable
Likely issues concerning professional negligence	High Court preferable

Figure 8: Starting proceedings: High Court or county court

Once issued, the claim form will either be 'served' by the court or, if the claimant requests, by the claimant. This will usually be done by sending it to the defendant by first class post, and where the defendant is resident or, if a limited company, has its registered office within England and Wales, it will be deemed served two days after posting.[8]

Alternatively where the defendant is an individual the claim form can be served by being posted through their letter box and, where the defendant is a company or a partnership, by being left at their registered office or principal place of business. The claim form must be accompanied by the prescribed 'response pack'.

Particulars of claim

Appendix 4 comprises a sample claim form and particulars of claim. While these are intended to illustrate the typical terms of these documents, obviously in particular cases there is no substitute for appropriate advice.

The sample claim form in Appendix 4 says 'see particulars of claim attached'. The Civil Procedure Rules provide various circumstances in which particulars of claim should or should not be served with the claim form. As a rule of thumb, with fee claims, the claim form should be accompanied by particulars of claim.

CPR Part 16 sets out the formal requirements of the particulars which can be summarised as follows:

- a concise statement of the facts on which the claimant relies;
- if the claimant is seeking interest a statement to that effect and the basis on which interest is claimed, for example, under the contract or by statute;
- a clear statement of the relief sought, for example, a specific sum of money;
- a statement of truth.[9]

From Appendix 4 it will be noted that the particulars set out the following:

- the appointment between the parties;
- the critical terms, particularly those dealing with payment;
- the failure to pay sums (despite demands for payment);
- the entitlement to interest;
- the sum claimed.

It is also sensible to annex copies of all documents referred to in the particulars of claim.

Acknowledgement of service and defence

After service of the claim form and the particulars of claim the defendant has 14 days in which to file an acknowledgement of service and then a further 14 days to file a defence. If the defendant feels it appropriate, they may wish to submit a CPR Part 20 claim – the new term for a counterclaim. If the claimant believes this is merely a tactic to unreasonably complicate and delay the action it is open to them to argue that this should be dealt with separately and subsequently. In support of this contention, it is sensible to refer to the existence (if the appointment utilises one of the standard forms) of a clause restricting the right of set-off, for example, clause 5.11 in SFA/99.

The acknowledgement of service is simply a statement to the effect that the defendant contests the proceedings. The defence is subject to the same rules governing the particulars of claim. The importance of this is that the defendant is obliged to set out their detailed contentions; they cannot simply deny the

Getting Paid

claim and leave it to the claimant to prove their contentions.

The parties are at liberty to agree an extension of time of up to 28 days for the service of a defence; beyond that the defendant must apply to the court. In the type of claim with which we are concerned, the court will take some persuasion that any more time needs to be granted.

Allocation

Once a defence has been served the court sends each party a document called an 'allocation questionnaire' (the AQ) and will specify a date by which it is to be returned completed to the court. The AQ sets out a series of questions about the case such as the sums at stake and the witnesses the parties intend to call in support of their contentions. It also allows the parties to state whether they intend to apply for summary judgement (see at p.93) or whether they wish the case to be stayed for a period of time to allow them to attempt to settle, together with any other information which the parties consider necessary to allow the court properly to manage the proceedings. The parties should also state whether any of the pre-action protocols (briefly considered above) apply to the case. The parties are obliged to co-operate with each other in relation to the production of the answers to the AQ.

Upon receipt of the AQ the court will allocate the dispute to a 'track'. For our purposes these can conveniently be divided as follows:

- the small claims track, for claims with a monetary value under £5,000;
- the fast track, where the sum at stake is below £15,000;
- the multi-track, for all other claims.

The guidelines above are not exhaustive or exclusive. In determining which track to allocate, the court will take into account the following:

- the sums at stake, including the value of any counterclaim;
- the complexity of the issues including the need for any expert evidence and whether any questions of law are raised;
- the amount of any oral evidence and the likely length of any hearing;

- the views of the parties.

The court notifies the parties of the track to which it has allocated the matter and, if it has allocated it to the small claims track, issues standard directions.

The small claims track
This will generally be used where the claim is for less than £5,000 and any hearing will last less than a day. The court will fix a date for the hearing of the matter which will be not less than 21 days in the future, and will direct that not less than 14 days before that date the parties shall serve on each other all evidence, whether in the form of documents, witness statements or other matters on which they intend to rely. If a party intends to call expert evidence (the necessity for which is dealt with at p.92) the permission of the court is required. The hearing is in public, is informal and the general rule is that a party will not be entitled to recover their costs.

The small claims track is therefore useful when dealing with very simple matters which can be dealt with in a short and informal procedure. It is ideal where the parties want to settle their differences quickly and generally without extensive recourse to lawyers. While the parties are permitted to be represented, it is not unusual for parties to be unrepresented. Normally, costs are not allowable in the small claims track. However, if SFA/99 or CE/99 have been used, it is open to the architect to argue that, if their claim is successful, costs both for any legal advice and for their own time should be paid as they are contractual entitlements under clause 9.6.

The fast track
Where the court allocates the matter to the fast track it will give directions for the management of the case and will set a timetable culminating in a trial date (or trial window, a period of up to three weeks within which the trial will take place). The rules state that the standard period between giving directions and the trial will be no more than 30 weeks. It is to be noted that in the fast track the court has specific powers to limit the costs recoverable by a party at trial and it is anticipated that in the near future all costs of fast track proceedings will be subject to a fixed scale.

Getting Paid

The courts have been at pains to stress that the success of the fast track depends upon the observance by the parties of pre-action protocols of the type described above and of the willingness of the parties to co-operate in identifying and narrowing issues. In allocating matters to the fast track the courts have also stressed that it is to be used where the trial length is envisaged as being no more than a day and that oral evidence is to be confined to one expert per party and that wherever possible the evidence of witnesses of fact is to be written. Time available for cross-examination of witnesses will be strictly limited by the court. In giving directions the court will address:

- disclosure of documents (see at p.97);
- service of witness statements; and
- expert evidence.

The rules anticipate that the parties will be obliged to disclose all documents directly relevant to their case and that in advance of trial they will exchange written statements setting out the basis of their contentions. Not less than eight weeks before the date fixed for trial the parties are obliged to submit a listing questionnaire stating that all matters necessary to bring the matter to trial have been done. As soon as possible after submission of the listing questionnaire the court will fix a trial date if it has not done so already and will issue a trial timetable. This will set out strict guillotines on the amount of time available for opening statements, witnesses (if cross-examination is permitted) and closing submissions.

Most simple fee recovery claims ought to be capable of being dealt with under the fast track. The limiting factor tends to be the existence of a threatened counterclaim. This may have the effect of convincing the court that in fact the matter ought to be dealt with under the more complex multi-track (see at p.91). There is, however, no reason why the claimant should not submit that in fact the claim is a simple matter and capable of being swiftly dealt with under the fast track and that any issue raised by the counterclaim can more conveniently be dealt with separately. The claimant's prospects of success in this submission will depend on individual circumstances, and to a large extent upon being able to show that claim and counterclaim can be severed, but there is some empirical evidence which suggests that the courts are becoming more willing to adopt this approach in appropriate circumstances.

The multi-track

All claims not allocated to the small claims or the fast track will be dealt with in the multi-track. Larger or more complex fee recovery claims will be allocated to this track.

In allocating a fee recovery matter to the multi-track, the court will almost always fix a date for a case management conference (CMC). This is a relatively informal hearing at which the court deals with timetabling and procedural matters, collectively termed 'case management'. The court stipulates that where the parties are legally represented the CMC must be attended by someone from the relevant law firm authorised to make decisions and with sufficient familiarity with the case to deal with any matters likely to arise.

The directions given by the court will include disclosure of documents, exchange of witness statements, expert evidence and meetings of experts, and the fixing of a trial date, the length of the trial and the order in which witnesses are to be heard and any time limits on cross-examination of witnesses. The court will also, where it considers it apt, fix dates for further case management conferences and pre-trial conferences and will take such measures as it considers apt to ensure that the matter is dealt with efficiently and proportionately. These can include ordering the parties (or in the case of limited companies, directors of the company) to attend before the court and where it considers that its directions have been breached without good cause can make orders that specific costs shall be paid by one party to the other forthwith. Within the Technology and Construction Court, where the determination of architect's fee recovery claims will be dealt with only in exceptional circumstances, the judges have adopted what might be termed a policy of enlightened interventionism – making it clear that they see their job as ensuring that matters are dealt with in a manner appropriate to the dispute in question and ensuring that once directions are given, they are meant to be observed.

Getting Paid

Expert evidence

In the majority of fee claims, particularly where the fast track is allocated, there will be little scope for expert evidence. The question is generally whether a particular sum is due or not and this will usually be a question of fact. In rare cases there may be a more difficult issue, such as whether a particular work stage has been reached and if so whether a particular fee installment is therefore due, in which case there may be scope for expert evidence.

In these cases, the architect would be well advised to participate in the selection of an expert witness to ensure that they are satisfied that the expert understands the issues involved and is sympathetic to the architect's position. (However, see at p.93 about the necessary independence of experts.)

The court's permission will be needed for expert evidence to be called. Particularly in the fast track, the court will encourage the use of a court-appointed joint expert. The present trend is that the court will permit the parties to have their own experts in circumstances where there is a genuinely difficult question on which at the CMC the parties are able to indicate a difference of view which requires the court to determine the issue.

In these circumstances the court will require the experts to meet on a without prejudice basis in order to attempt to agree facts and narrow issues. As indicated above, the court will also direct that experts' reports should be exchanged well in advance of the hearing. Where possible the court has sought not only to discourage the excessive use of experts but to encourage the scope of expert evidence to be limited to those matters where it is really required. In fee recovery cases it will be the case that expert evidence will be the exception rather than the rule in most cases.

In recent times there has also been an increasing emphasis placed on the role played by experts. It has been stressed that the expert is there to assist the court rather than simply to boost the client's case. With this in mind the practice has developed for experts to provide a declaration to the effect that they understand the nature of their obligations. It has also been common practice for experts to annex to their reports a copy of their instructions, so that it can be seen that they have not been instructed to 'slant' their opinion. There have been a number of high profile cases in which the courts have perceived that the expert on one side has been unduly keen to promote the client's position, sometimes at the expense of the truth, and the criticism meted out to such experts has been withering.

It is also becoming increasingly common for the courts to appoint a single joint expert to assist the court rather than to appear on behalf of one of the parties. This practice is still in its infancy and while its attractions are obvious it remains to be seen whether it really will simplify the process of providing expert evidence to the court.

Summary judgement

Part 24 of the CPR provides that at any point after filing of the acknowledgement of service, either party can apply for summary judgement. As the name suggests, summary judgement means that the court is entitled to make a ruling on the whole of the case or any specific issue where it considers either that the claimant has no real prospect of succeeding at trial or the defendant has no real prospect of successfully defending the action.

It will be appreciated that in fee recovery claims this is frequently an option which the claimant will wish to consider. Where the real issue is simply that the defendant does not want to pay, or that the relationship between the parties has broken down, it will often be an effective tactic. Additionally, following the introduction of the Civil Procedure Rules the court has shown itself more willing to adopt a robust attitude than was often the case in former times. The procedure is simple and is illustrated in Figure 9.

Getting Paid

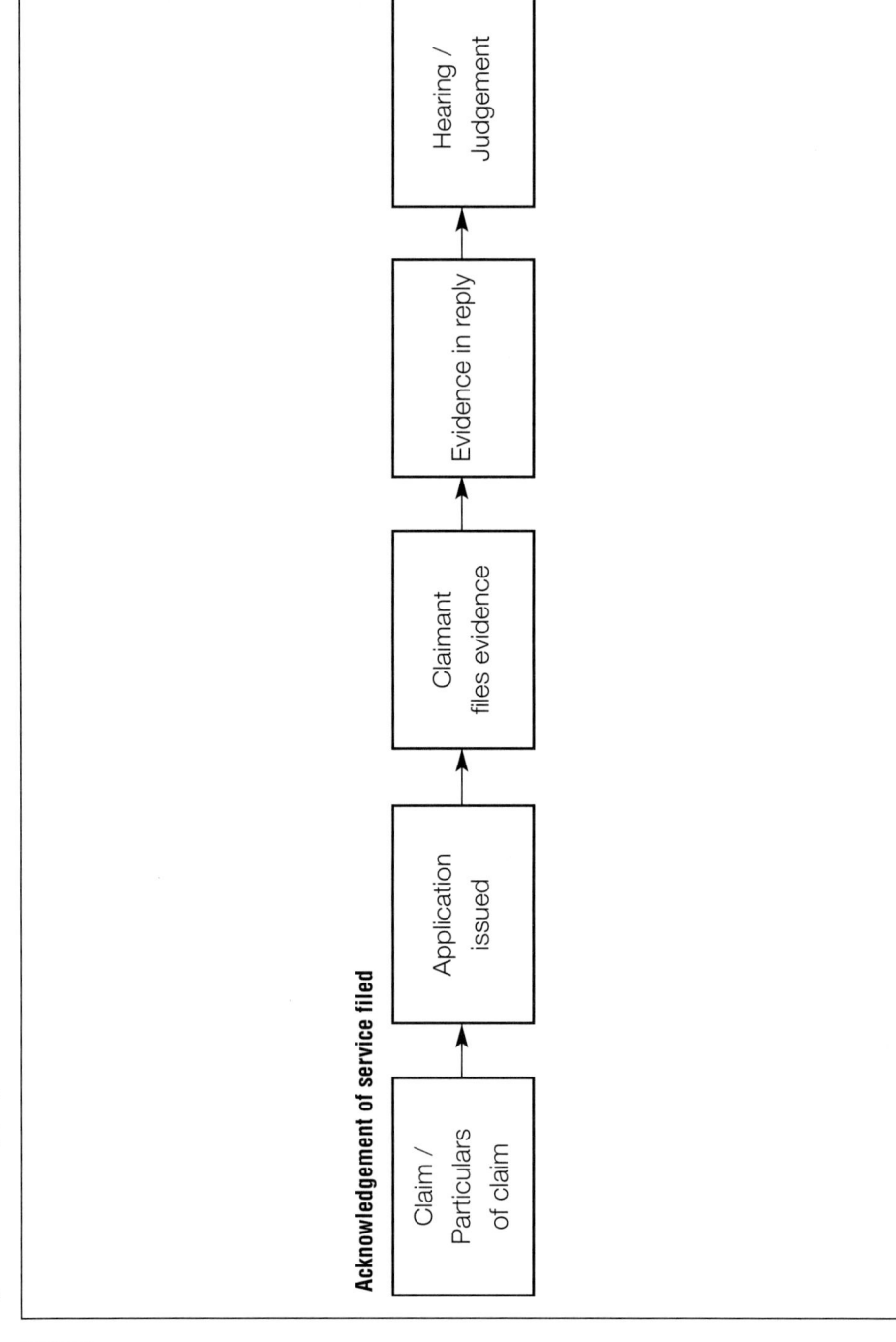

Figure 9: Summary judgement

Litigation and arbitration

The claimant issues an application and the court fixes a hearing date a minimum of 14 days later. When serving the application notice on the defendant the claimant must serve all evidence on which they intend to rely. In the case of an application by the claimant (which will generally be the case in fee recovery claims), this will comprise a witness statement which will set out the basis of the claim and must include a statement to the effect that there is no realistic prospect of the defendant defending the action, together with all relevant documents. The defendant should serve its evidence in reply a minimum of seven days before the hearing date. There will not usually be oral evidence except in exceptional circumstances (and this will be particularly rare in fee recovery cases). At the hearing the parties will make submissions and the court will make its decision.

The court may give summary judgement for the whole or part of the claim, or may reject the application. It may also take an intermediate approach, that is to say it may allow the defendant to continue to defend the matter on certain conditions, most frequently that of requiring the defendant to pay some or all of the sum claimed into the court's bank account. This will often be done where it considers the defence to be shadowy or insubstantial or where it considers that while the defendant may be able to prove its claim at trial, it is improbable or difficult. This will be a frequent approach in fee recovery claims.

Preliminary issues
Sometimes, in the interests of expediency, the court will be asked to give a judgement on a key issue on which the whole case depends, for example, whether there is indeed a contract. Such a hearing reduces the need – and cost – of arguing subsidiary issues until the preliminary issue is decided.

Security for costs
One of the problems facing the claimant of modest means is the provision of the rules which allows the defendant to apply for security for costs. In simple terms, where the court is satisfied that if the defendant is successful they may be unable to enforce a costs order, the court may order the claimant to provide security for those costs. Generally this will take the form of an order that the

Getting Paid

claimant should pay a sum of money into the court's bank account or provide a bond as a condition of continuing with the claim.

Where SFA/99 has been used, an arbitrator is barred by clause 9.5.3 from granting security for costs. As yet there is no decided authority on whether such a provision will be effective. Of course, the fact that the parties have agreed in their contract that security for costs will not be sought or granted will be very persuasive to a court or arbitrator.

In the majority of claims dealt with in this book, this will only be relevant where the claimant is a limited company. Although the rules contain certain provisions for individuals to provide security, those will seldom apply in the types of claims with which we are concerned.

Accordingly, faced with a claim for fees, where the architect is a limited company, the first thing the defendant will do in most cases is to order a company search and investigate the solvency and liquidity of the claimant. In many cases where the architect is a small business operating on an overdraft, the accounts will justify the contention that if the claim is unsuccessful the architect will be unable to pay the defendant's costs.

The right to security is discretionary; the mere fact that the defendant can bring themselves within the financial grounds set out in the previous paragraph does not mean that the court will make an order for security unless satisfied that it is the appropriate course to take. In making that decision the court has a number of guiding principles which it will consider:

- **prospects of success:** if the claimant's case is very clear and the application is simply a ploy to frustrate it, the court may exercise its discretion in favour of the claimant. In general, though, the court will not enquire deeply into the merits of the claim;
- **time of making the application:** generally the earlier the claim for security is made, the greater the likelihood that discretion will be exercised in the defendant's favour;

- **the existence of a substantial offer to settle the claim:** clearly, if this has been done, the likelihood that the claimant's action will succeed is significantly greater and the likelihood of an order being made diminishes. Conversely, if there has been a CPR Part 36 offer or payment into court of the type discussed at p.98, it might be considered by the court that the defendant has been mindful of their risk and has sought to shift the burden of risk onto the claimant, and this will increase the likelihood of an order being made;
- **conduct of the parties:** where the impecuniosity of the claimant has been brought about by the defendant, the court will be less willing to exercise its discretion;
- **likelihood that a successful application for security will stifle a genuine claim:** although this point is invariably taken by claimants it is rare that it succeeds if none of the previous points have been resolved in favour of the claimant.

In Chapter 9, consideration is given to legal expenses insurance. The greater availability of legal expenses insurance and the fact that the obtaining of legal expenses insurance will effectively thwart applications for security in most instances should be seen as the most likely means of heading off an order for security.

Disclosure

Prior to the Woolf Reforms, the procedure of discovery existed whereby the parties were obliged to serve lists setting out all of the documents which they had in their possession, custody or power and which related to any matter in dispute. The parties then had the right to inspect one another's documents. The effect of this was to produce an often lengthy process of inspecting documents and seeking discovery of further documents. The Woolf Reforms sought to limit this by setting limits on the scope of disclosure (as it is now called) and in all but the multi-track by discouraging extensive attritional battles over the scope of documents to be disclosed. Within matters assigned to the multi-track it is clear that not much has changed and in complex matters considerable time and cost will still be expended on lengthy trawls through documents. The justification for this is that in complex disputes there is merit in

Getting Paid

compelling the parties to adopt a 'cards on the table' approach and it may be the case that within an opponent's documents there will be something akin to the 'smoking gun' which will significantly damage their case. In most fee recovery cases except the largest and most complex, lengthy disclosure exercises are almost always to be discouraged.

In any event, it will generally be the architect's files which are relied on as the architect is likely to have kept the most detailed records in the course of carrying out the works. It is therefore important that these files are clear and in complete order before an action is commenced.

Part 36 offers and payments into court

The courts encourage settlement and as a matter of policy seek to discourage litigants from holding out for the last penny. The courts have therefore devised a means of encouraging parties to settle their differences in a way which gives incentives for settlement without forcing the parties to compromise the position they are adopting in the litigation. This is now enshrined in Part 36 of the Civil Procedure Rules. Part 36 offers, sometimes called 'Calderbank offers', are an important tactic for encouraging settlement.

The basic principles are as follows (and it will be noted that slightly different considerations prevail for claimants and defendants):

- At any time up to 21 days before trial a party may serve on the other party an offer expressed to be 'without prejudice save as to costs' in which they offer to pay the other party a sum of money in settlement of the whole or any particular part of their claim. The existence of that offer is not communicated to the trial judge until he or she has dealt with all matters except costs.
- In the case of an offer being made by a defendant after commencement of proceedings that offer should usually (except in very exceptional circumstances) be combined with the payment of the principal sum into the court's bank account.
- The offer should be precise in its terms and in particular should stipulate how interest is to be treated and what provision is being made in respect of costs. As a general rule, where an offer is made to settle the whole claim, that offer

should be expressed as an offer to pay a principal sum plus costs to be assessed in default of agreement.[10] Where the offer is to settle particular heads of claim the offer should stipulate which claims it applies to and that the offeror also offers to pay the costs of those claims.
- The offer is open for acceptance for 21 days from the date on which it is made. If accepted, the action (or, as the case may be, all the claims to which it relates) is settled on the terms set out in the offer – usually the payment of the sum offered plus costs.
- Thereafter the offer can be accepted on terms that while the offeror will pay the offeree's costs up to the date of the offer, after that date the offeree must pay the offeror's costs.
- If at trial the offeree recovers more than the sum offered, the offer has no effect – the usual rules apply in relation to costs. However. if a claimant fails to beat a defendant's offer they will usually be ordered to pay the defendant's costs after the date of the offer. If, in the case of an offer by a claimant, the claimant recovers more than the sum offered, the defendant will be ordered not only to pay the claimant's costs but to pay interest at a punitive rate on those costs, currently 7 per cent over base rate.

The key points are summarised in Figure 10.

---

1. **Offer by defendant: considerations for claimant:**
- Does this offer represent a 'toe in the water' by the defendant?
- Does it reflect (a) an optimistic or (b) a pessimistic view of the defendant's prospects?
- Does it reflect the risks the claimant has identified in continuing the action?
- What risk does the claimant run if they refuse the offer?
- Should the claimant make a counterclaim offer?

2. **Offer by claimant: considerations for defendant:**
   As above but also:
- Timing of offer: what does this say about the claimant's case?
- How does this offer correspond with the defendant's own perspective on the risks in the action?

Figure 10: CPR Part 36 offers: points to consider

Getting Paid

It will be appreciated that this is a potent tool both for encouraging the parties to settle but also to take a candid look at their prospects of success. In the context of fee claims, the defendant has the option to consider just what the architect claimant is likely to recover, or indeed what sum might be sufficient to tempt him to 'take the money and run'. For the claimant the ability to make an offer (which is an innovation introduced in 1998) allows them to send a clear signal that they have considered the extent of their claim and their prospects and if the offer is carefully pitched will place the defendant under pressure either to settle or face a financial penalty if they proceed.

Tactically the existence of the Part 36 machinery encourages the parties to avoid holding out on the basis of points of principle. Because fee recovery claims are often dogged by strong feelings there is frequent reluctance on either side to make an offer because this is perceived as capitulation. The availability of this procedure allows the parties to make an offer of compromise on the basis of sound commercial principles rather than emotional ones. Although it is tempting to regard a low offer – or any offer which appears below the other's prospects of recovery – as an insult, calculated to slight, this is to be resisted at all costs. While it may be that the effect of the offer is to add insult to injury, the prudent litigator will ask why such an offer has been made; has a low offer been made primarily because the claim advanced is a poor one, or alternatively, does it merely suggest that there is a difference in opinion between the parties as to their prospects. These are issues which require careful thought.

Service out of the jurisdiction
An unwelcome discovery for any party is to find that although negotiations had taken place with a known individual, the contract has actually been concluded with an offshore company, registered in a tax haven.[11] This raises two problems: first, there is the question of service of proceedings (which is dealt with here) and secondly there is the question of whether any judgement can be enforced.

Litigation and arbitration

In the case of service out of the jurisdiction, the claimant faces two further problems. Except where the defendant has instructed lawyers to accept service of the proceedings, the claimant will face the task of serving the proceedings on the defendant in the place where they are resident or registered. Furthermore, except in the case of a limited number of countries,[12] the claimant faces the task of obtaining permission of the court to serve proceedings out of the jurisdiction.

While the task of obtaining leave to serve out of the jurisdiction is not inherently complex, provided that the requirements of the CPR are met, and while service in the relevant jurisdiction is similarly an exercise in ensuring that relevant procedures are met, both of these requirements add expense and complexity to the process of pursuing claims and may serve to discourage claimants.

Where the defendant has instructed lawyers and these lawyers nonetheless indicate that they are not instructed to accept service of proceedings and that the claimant must therefore go through the process of obtaining leave and serving out of the jurisdiction, it is open to the claimant in seeking permission to ask the court to order that the costs of serving out of the jurisdiction should be borne by the defendant (who should in the interests of proportionality have agreed that the lawyers would accept service). Architects would be well advised not to accept a commission from an entity not resident in Britain without securing an advance payment greater than the anticipated interim fee invoices.

Arbitration procedure
Introduction
It is tempting to think that arbitration is no more than litigation in the private sector. Prior to the Arbitration Act 1996 there was some justification for this view. The effect of the Act, however, has been to introduce a greater flexibility into the arbitration process such that the parties and the arbitrator can tailor the proceedings to suit the needs of the dispute. Indeed, sections 33 and 40 of the Act impose duties on both the arbitrator and the parties to adopt procedures suitable to the circumstances of the case so as to provide a fair means of

Getting Paid

determining the dispute and to do all things necessary for the proper and expeditious conduct of the proceedings.

Arbitrations can therefore be conducted in any manner which the parties, and more particularly the arbitrator, consider appropriate to the circumstances. There is therefore no pre-determined procedure to constrain the parties other than the following:

- the arbitrator must conduct the proceedings in accordance with the principles of natural justice;
- in practice, that requirement usually means that the arbitrator must not hear representations from one party which the other party is not made aware of, and must not accept in evidence any material from one party which is not disclosed to the other;
- the arbitrator will usually be immune from being sued by either party in connection with any matter arising out of the exercise of the arbitrator's powers.

What is very clear is that the parties need to address themselves at the commencement of the matter to the most appropriate way to conduct proceedings. Accordingly, it is not intended in this section to go through the conduct of arbitration proceedings in the same detail as that given over to litigation above because this is likely to change from one matter to the next. Depending upon the circumstances of the case, the matter may be dealt with on the basis of no more than a consideration of the material documents or something which is tantamount to a full-scale high court trial on the multi-track, complete with experts, witnesses and cross-examination. Instead, some consideration is given to fee recovery issues and how these can most appropriately be dealt with in arbitration proceedings.

Fee recovery claims in arbitration

Arbitration is not subject to the same pre-action protocols as litigation. There is no doubt, however, that it is wise for the claimant to write an appropriate letter before commencing proceedings, if only to give the other party the opportunity to set out his reasons for non-payment in the event that these are not already well known. If this does not produce a result, formal arbitration proceedings are commenced by serving on the other party a notice to concur in the appointment of an arbitrator.

In cases where there is no threatened counterclaim it will often be possible for fee recovery claims to be dealt with extremely simply. Having served notice to concur in the appointment of an arbitrator, the parties will either agree to a particular person being appointed or they will seek a nomination to be made by the body named in the appointment.

Upon appointment the arbitrator will generally convene a preliminary meeting and if persuaded will direct that the matter should be dealt with by way of a documents only or summary procedure. This may mean that the arbitrator will determine the matter solely on the basis of the documents put to them or following a hearing at which oral submissions are put to the arbitrator, without in either case the parties having to call witnesses or adduce evidence. Figure 11 illustrates the course which a documents only arbitration might take. A comparison with the procedure for adjudication described in the next chapter will show how very similar they are.

It will clearly generally be in the interests of the claimant to assert that the matter really is sufficiently straightforward that it can be dealt with in this manner, and it will generally suit the respondent to assert that in reality the matter raises sufficiently complex issues that some more elaborate procedure, involving experts, witnesses and the use of cross-examination is apt. It is therefore incumbent upon the claimant and their advisers to ensure that at the earliest possible stage in proceedings they are able to marshal their case sufficiently cogently to convince the arbitrator that a summary procedure is apt, perhaps throwing in the point that if in fact there are matters which need subsequent and more complex investigation (which will almost always mean a counterclaim which has been threatened but is not yet articulated in any meaningful way), that this should be dealt with separately and subsequently.

Getting Paid

Figure 11: Documents only arbitration

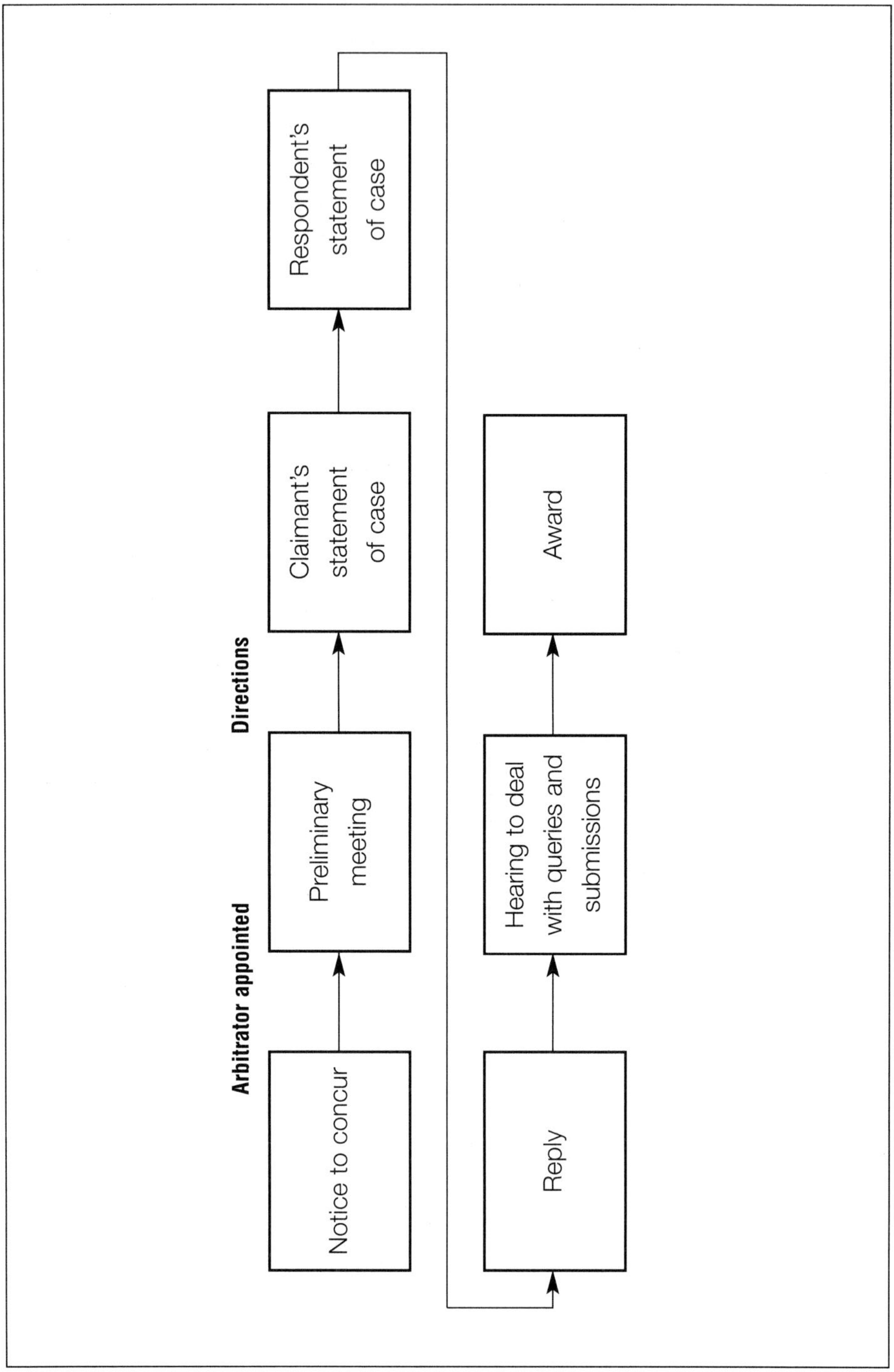

It would be wrong to believe that failure to persuade the arbitrator to adopt this procedure is fatal to the claimant's prospects of success. However, claimants may often encounter a reluctance on the part of arbitrators to adopting a summary procedure except in clear cases, and the effect of this will be to make proceedings slower and more costly, which will seldom be to the claimant's advantage. It is worth reflecting that an inability to convince the arbitrator to adopt a summary procedure will often be as a result of some failure to be able to point to records which convincingly support the fee claim or which suggest that there is some underlying argument over whether the sums claimed are properly payable, as discussed in previous chapters.

Costs

Prior to the Arbitration Act 1996 and the Woolf Reforms, the general rule in litigation and arbitration was that costs followed the event. This expression meant in simple terms that the winning party was entitled to have their costs – or a large proportion of them – paid by the losing party. Even where 'winning' meant that the party recovered no more than a nominal sum, that party could expect to receive the majority of their costs from their opponent.

However, it should be noted that such costs do not normally include an element for the architect's own time, which can be considerable in pursuing a fee recovery action, unless by agreement between the parties such as that set out in SFA/99 (see at p.32). The effect of this was that costs frequently deterred parties from starting claims; and once proceedings had begun, parties often found themselves locked into proceedings in which the costs had come to outweigh the sums at stake. This was often a problem with fee claims, in which the defendant's initial decision to defend the matter 'on principle' frequently turned into a decision to defend the matter at any price because they could not afford to do anything else faced with a potentially ruinous costs bill.

The only real winners from this were lawyers. Matters were made worse by the fact that the winning party would invariably only recover a proportion of their costs from the loser, leaving the winning party with an often sizeable element of irrecoverable costs which they would still be liable to pay to their lawyers.

Getting Paid

This occurred less as a consequence of the greed of lawyers in private practice but more as a result of the administration by the courts of the process (called taxation of costs) by which a party recovered costs from an opponent.

To recover costs in litigation a party was obliged to produce a bill in a particular detailed form, setting out each item which they sought to recover. The bill was then scrutinised by a court official called a taxing master, and the opposing party was entitled to raise objections to any specific items, and if the taxing master so decided, particular items were reduced or 'taxed off'. The resulting total was the sum which could be recovered. The rule of thumb was that taxed costs were generally between 25 and 40 per cent less than the sum which a party would be liable to pay their lawyers.

The procedure in arbitration aped that in litigation with the added disadvantage that since most arbitrators were understandably less familiar with costs matters than taxing masters the procedure tended to be unpredictable.

This unsatisfactory state of affairs has been radically overhauled following the Arbitration Act 1996 and the Woolf Reforms. The approach taken by both courts and arbitrators can now be summed up in a single word – proportionality – and the clear intention of both has been to make costs issues, so far as possible, a subordinate rather than a dominant part of the process of dispute resolution. Consideration of the Civil Procedure Rules and the Arbitration Act 1996 leaves three clear impressions:

- costs may be used by the courts as a tool to punish parties whose behaviour is at odds with the overriding objective (or in the case of arbitration the objectives summarised above);
- wherever possible costs issues are to be dealt with summarily and simply, and the sort of lengthy codas experienced in many cases while costs were sorted out are to be avoided except in extreme instances while arrangements designed to limit or simplify costs are to be encouraged;
- in making costs orders the courts will give effect to the reality of the result: if one party has succeeded on some but not all of their claim, the costs ordered will generally reflect this.

Litigation and arbitration

Accordingly, the previous notion that if a party recovered £1 they would be entitled to their costs is no longer the case. Furthermore, if in the course of the matter a party has behaved unreasonably or unco-operatively (since not to co-operate with the other parties is now one of the worst crimes that can be committed), this will be reflected in the costs order. Additionally, during the course of the proceedings the court is empowered to punish particular infractions of the rules by making summary costs orders and directing that the sums which it assesses as being attributable to that matter should actually be paid, and that the solicitors involved should inform their client that this has been directed.

In the case of claims for fees the new rules should act to the benefit of the claimant architect provided always that the claimant has commenced the claim with their 'tackle in order', i.e. having carefully worked out what is being claimed and having organised the material needed to prove that claim. In cases where the opposing party's basis for defending the action is shadowy or apparently insubstantial or where the defence to the matter appears to involve prevarication, the courts and arbitrators have the power to reflect this in costs orders in a way which did not previously exist.

The new rules will, however, work against the claimant in cases where the sum recovered is a small proportion of that originally claimed or where particular heads of claim fail. In those circumstances the claimant may well find themselves recovering only a proportion of their costs, and facing a substantial irrecoverable element of costs.

In cases where SFA/99 is used the matter is simpler. Under clause 9.6.1, the client indemnifies the architect in respect of legal and other costs including the architect's own time in pursuing a fee recovery action if the architect obtains a judgement of the court or an arbitrator's award in their favour for recovery of fees or expenses under the agreement. Such an indemnity means that the architect should recover a greater proportion of their costs than under the normal taxation procedure.

Getting Paid

Endnotes:

1. The rules governing civil procedure are contained in the Civil Procedure Rules, the published version of which is edited by a panel of judges, district judges and high court masters. Volume 1 contains the rules themselves while volume 2 contains precedents for forms of wording, copies of relevant forms and useful statutes. Combined they occupy approximately 20 cm of shelf space. They are supplemented by frequent updates and amendments.

2. See respectively the *Report of the Department Advisory Committee* chaired by Lord Mustill (the Mustill Report) and the interim and final reports *Access to Justice* by Lord Woolf.

3. © Crown Copyright. An up-to-date and complete version of the Civil Procedure Rules can be found at www.lcd.gov.uk/index.htm

4. Presumably the 'the' in the title of the Protocol is superfluous and in due course will be removed. The typographical error is unfortunate because it detracts from a document which was produced by the Lord Chancellor's Department following lengthy consultation with lawyers engaged in these types of disputes. A full version of the Protocol is available at www.lcd.gov.uk/index.htm © Crown Copyright.

5. The Protocol does not apply to claims seeking summary judgement or claims seeking the enforcement of adjudication decisions (see Chapter 8).

6. The claim form in prescribed form N1 is available from TSO and from most court offices. www.hmso.gov.uk

7. Until 1998 known as the Official Referee's Court, the court office is located on the third floor of St Dunstan's House, 133-137 Fetter Lane, London, EC4A 1HD. Where proceedings are issued outside London they can also be issued as Technology and Construction Court business.

8. See at p.100 on service out of the jurisdiction where the defendant is located outside England and Wales.

9. This is an innovation brought in by the Civil Procedure Rules; the statement of truth can be signed by either the claimant or their solicitor.

10. Assessment of costs is dealt with at p.105.

11. All too frequently this question is not really addressed at the time the appointment is concluded. Of course, there is nothing wrong with the client conducting business through a tax vehicle, but at the very least it is helpful for the architect to be aware of the ramifications of this.

12. In broad terms, permission to serve out of the jurisdiction is not required where the defendant is resident in an EU state (except Denmark) or in a country which is a member of EFTA (european free trade association).

8 Adjudication

Introduction

Although adjudication will not generally be available for disputes over private dwellings, for the majority of other appointments there is a statutory right to adjudication provided by the HGCRA 1996, section 108 where the appointment was entered after 30 April 1998. At its simplest, adjudication can be defined as a mechanism whereby a third party is appointed to rule on disputes within a timetable not exceeding 28 days. Such a decision is binding unless or until altered by subsequent litigation or arbitration.

Although the introduction of such a quick method of dealing with disputes was greeted with some misgivings, the majority of those involved in the resolution of construction disputes have come to the view that adjudication is in many cases an efficient means of producing (at the very least) an interim result, which often in fact turns out to be a permanent resolution of the dispute. Although adjudication is only binding until the decision is revised by later proceedings, in many cases it provides the parties with the equivalent of their 'day in court' – the chance to air their grievances before a neutral third party. Frequently, even if the result goes against them, they will conclude – often very wisely – that there is no merit in pursuing matters to a higher tribunal where there is no guarantee of a different result.

In the context of fee claims the prospect of achieving a resolution of the dispute within 28 days is obviously attractive. One of the problems with litigation and arbitration identified in the previous chapter is the time which can be taken, and the risk that the determined opponent can, even now, cause such proceedings to be spun out over months and sometimes years.

Since many of the hardest fought fee disputes concern works to private dwellings, the absence of the right to adjudication for such disputes is unfortunate.[1] It is, of course, open to the architect, while negotiating the appointment, to suggest the inclusion of a right to adjudication.[2] Alternatively, if and when a dispute occurs, it is open to the architect to suggest that this would be the most efficient means to resolve the dispute. Alternatively, if the parties have agreed that their relationship will be governed by the terms of CE/99 and SFA/99, clause 9.2 provides that any dispute can be dealt with by adjudication. Remember though, in the decision in *Picardi* v *Cuniberti*, the architect sought to rely on the incorporation of this clause without having discussed it with his client. The court refused to hold that this clause was incorporated into the agreement between the parties.

The advantages

First and foremost, the attraction of any system of dispute resolution which allows the parties to proceed from commencement to an enforceable decision in a matter of weeks rather than months cannot be over-stressed. This has a number of facets:

- Speed is obviously linked to cost: adjudication is generally a cheap way of resolving disputes.
- Although there is inevitably a trade off between speed of decision-making and the quality of the decision, this is more of a concern in larger and more complex claims. In most architect's fee claims it will be unusual for the quality of the decision to be affected adversely by the tight timetable, and as considered at p.115 it may in some cases be an advantage.
- The degree of disruption, particularly for a small practice, will be significantly less where the timetable occupies weeks rather than months or years.

Secondly, adjudication has been designed to allow the matter to be conducted while permitting the parties to continue with the works; the prospect of the parties preserving a working relationship is obviously greater where they have been involved in a matter occupying a month or so and which has been conducted along relatively informal lines.

Thirdly, adjudication is flexible and informal. The various sets of procedural rules for adjudication all encourage the adjudicator and the parties to adopt procedures most suited to the quick and efficient disposal of the matter. By way of example, in the Procedural Rules published by the Technology and Construction Court Solicitors Association (TeCSA), it is provided that the adjudicator shall take the lead in ascertaining the facts and the law[3] and the Rules provide a lengthy and non-exclusive list of ways in which the adjudicator may conduct the proceedings, essentially providing that, within the over-all constraint of acting fairly, the adjudicator has a free hand.

Adjudication

Rule 15 in the same set of rules contains the important provision that where possible the adjudicator shall decide the dispute in accordance with the legal entitlements of the parties, but where this is not clear the adjudicator shall decide the matter as he or she considers fair and just within the context of a quick and efficient method of dispute resolution. While this provision has given rise to controversy, it is clear that it was the intention of the drafting committee that the process should not become bogged down in debate over legal minutiae and that the adjudicator should be free where appropriate to adopt a broad brush common sense approach.

In short, the attractions of adjudication are that it provides a quick, cheap and pragmatic approach to dispute resolution. The misgivings of professional indemnity insurers over adjudication have been addressed in Chapter 6. Experience suggests that these concerns have some justification, especially given the perverse results which adjudication has sometimes thrown up. However, as adjudication becomes more widely used, these misgivings are, to an extent, being addressed.

Finally, the following two considerations have sparked mixed views, but in the eyes of the authors are to be regarded as advantages of adjudication. The first is that all of the sets of procedural rules specify that while the adjudicator may order that his or her costs shall be borne by the parties in such proportion as the adjudicator shall direct, unless the parties agree otherwise the adjudicator shall not order one to pay the costs of the other. Clearly this means that the costs considerations referred to in Chapter 7 will not apply to adjudication. However, clause 9.2 of SFA/99 provides that the adjudicator may in his or her discretion direct the payment of legal costs and expenses to one party by another and may determine the amount of costs to be paid or may delegate the costs to an independent costs draftsman.

The second consideration is that most sets of rules provide that, in the absence of contrary agreement, the adjudicator shall not be obliged to publish reasons for the decision. While it is becoming commonplace for reasons to be required, it is surely an advantage where the parties agree to allow the adjudicator to form a decision without requiring that they produce something akin to a judgement.

Some disadvantages

The disadvantages of adjudication are much the same as the advantages, viewed from the opposite perspective. The risk with any quick, cheap and informal method of dispute resolution is that it can lead to decisions which would have been different had the parties and the adjudicator had lesser constraints upon their time.

This is made worse by the fact that all of the sets of procedural rules provide that the decision is final and binding until varied by subsequent proceedings; in other words, the right of appeal is very limited. The growing body of case law surrounding complaints about adjudicators' decisions allows certain cautionary lessons to be drawn:

- Where the adjudicator has simply got it wrong, the courts will be loath to interfere with the decision. (By 'getting it wrong' we mean that the adjudicator has been asked a question and has produced an answer to that question which appears to be misguided).
- However, where the adjudicator has answered a question which was not asked, the courts will decline to allow that decision to be enforced.
- The same will be true where the courts conclude that the contract was not one to which the HGCRA 1996 applied and there is no evidence that the parties had entered into some sort of ad hoc arrangement to adjudicate. As considered above, except where this has been carefully explained to the client (especially where the client is a private individual), the courts will be loath to uphold ad hoc agreements.[4]
- Finally, the courts will not allow the enforcement of a decision which has been procured by a serious procedural irregularity, particularly where that has occurred in circumstances which might demonstrate significant unfairness to one of the parties. Examples of this include instances where the adjudicator demonstrated clear bias against one of the parties and where the adjudicator appeared to take submissions from one party without allowing the other the right to reply.[5]

Adjudication

How adjudication works

Various sets of procedural rules exist for adjudication. It is open to the parties to agree in their contract to make use of one of these sets of rules. Where the contract does not specify a set of rules, the parties are obliged to use the procedural rules contained in the 'Scheme for Construction Contracts' published pursuant to the HGCRA 1996. While each set of rules has its own adherents, in reality each set of rules is similar.

Accordingly, the following description of the sequence of events in an adjudication, while based upon the rules contained in the Scheme for Construction Contracts, will be much the same whichever set of rules is used.

The starting point, as discussed above, is the existence of a dispute.[6] To commence an adjudication, the claimant serves notice on the opposing party (whether by letter or a more formal document headed 'notice of dispute' is not important) stating that a dispute has arisen, setting out with precision the nature of the dispute, and stating that the claimant is referring that dispute to adjudication (see Figure 12 overleaf).

Getting Paid

- Be careful to describe with precision what is in dispute. If the complaint is that fees have been sought and not paid, say so, identifying what and when and how the opposing party has contested the entitlement.
- Identify the issue which the adjudicator is to determine. Frequently this will flow automatically from the dispute identified.
- Remember that the adjudicator can only rule on the issue which has been put to them; if the matter is put too broadly (for example, 'the way in which the architect administered the building contract'), the opposing party is at liberty to put the whole of the project in issue. On the other hand, if too narrow (for example, 'my entitlement to £25,675.50 plus VAT, as applied for under application number 5') there is a risk that if the adjudicator finds that this precise sum is not due, they cannot award anything.
- In stating that a particular matter is being referred to adjudication, be precise. If it is expressed as 'and it is my intention to refer these matters to adjudication' it is open to the opposing party to say that while this may be intended in the future, it is not being done now.
- Remember that the area which gives rise to more problems than almost any other arises out of a failure properly to give notice of the matters in dispute.

Figure 12: Notice of adjudication: some points to watch

It may be that the appointment specifies an individual who is to act as adjudicator, or identifies a particular nominating body who will appoint an adjudicator. In the absence of such a provision, any of the adjudicator nominating bodies can be asked to appoint. Most will have a form which is to be completed and will require payment of a small fee, typically between £150 and £250 plus VAT. The form generally seeks details of the nature of the dispute, to enable the nominating body to select an adjudicator who has relevant experience.

Adjudication

Typically the adjudicator is to be appointed within three working days of the request for appointment. The adjudicator will contact the parties enclosing their terms for acting. Generally, an adjudicator's fees are capped at a maximum of £1,000 per day.

Within seven days of the appointment, the claimant (sometimes described as the 'referring party') must serve a referral notice. This sets out the claimant's case in detail, and should identify all matters relied upon and all documents to which they intend to make reference.[7] This should include experts' reports and witness statements. It is worth remembering that all relevant matters, positive and negative, should be identified and failure to do so entitles the adjudicator to draw an adverse inference.

- The tight time limits for adjudication make it advisable to ensure that the referral notice is complete at the time when the request for the appointment of the adjudicator is submitted. This allows the time constraints to work to the advantage of the claimant.
- Although a referral notice is not subject to the rules governing formal statements of case in arbitration and litigation, these do provide useful guidance – clarity and brevity are always virtues.
- Remember that the adjudicator will be coming to the matter afresh; he or she will not have the detailed knowledge of the matter which the parties have and it is a good discipline to ask whether a particular assertion will be understood by someone in that position.
- The requirement to deal with both favourable and unfavourable points can be problematic. Where it is known that a particular argument will be relied upon, this should be used as an opportunity to anticipate that argument and set out the counter-argument. Again the statement can be made to work in favour of the referring party who can, by anticipating the opponent's case, 'take the wind out of his sails'.

Figure 13: Referral notice: some tips

Getting Paid

It is also important to bear in mind that the ambit of the dispute is set by the adjudication notice and that the referral notice should not seek to raise matters not included within the scope of that notice.

Thereafter the adjudicator has a wide power to direct that the matter should be conducted as they consider apt. Almost invariably this will involve directing that the respondent should respond to the referral notice – to proceed otherwise would expose the adjudicator to the allegation that they had dealt unfairly with the matter.

The procedural rules provide a lengthy and non-exclusive list of the actions which the adjudicator may take in determining the dispute. These include:

- request any party to the contract to supply the adjudicator with such documents as they may reasonably require, or any written statement from any party supporting or supplementing any matter in the referral notice;
- decide on the language of the adjudication and order the translation of any document;
- meet and question any of the parties to the contract and their representatives;
- subject to obtaining any necessary consent, make any site visit the adjudicator considers appropriate;
- carry out any tests or experiments;
- obtain and consider such representations as the adjudicator may require and with the consent of the parties obtain or appoint experts, assessors or legal advisers;
- give directions for the timetable for the matter or limit the length of any submissions or oral representations.

A few examples

In short, the adjudicator is encouraged to be proactive in finding the best way to determine the matter:

- If the adjudicator considers it apt they can telephone and question either of the parties. However, the initiative for this should come from the adjudicator:

Adjudication

it is unwise of either of the parties to telephone the adjudicator without the express consent of the other.
- The adjudicator can convene hearings at which the parties' representatives debate the matters in issue, much as in an arbitration.
- The adjudicator can seek legal advice on any matter in issue. In this event it is sensible for the parties to ask for sight of the instructions to lawyers.
- Where appropriate the adjudicator can suggest that meetings be held at the site.

Of course, if one of the parties is strongly of the view that a particular approach should be adopted, they are at liberty to ask for it, and should be able to explain precisely why it is necessary for the proper disposal of the matter.

The adjudicator is obliged to produce their decision either 28 days after service of the referral notice, or 42 days after that date if the claimant requests, or after such longer period as the parties agree.

Applying this to architect's fee claims

The majority of fee claims are in themselves simple matters made more complex by the attempts of the client to put forward reasons for non-payment. In most instances a carefully worded adjudication notice will serve to limit the scope of the adjudication to the question of fees, and to exclude the issue of negligence. It is, of course, open to the opposing party to contend that the scope of the negligence is such that the architect's services are worthless and hence they should be paid nothing, but this is likely to be confined to the more acute cases, where the wisdom of seeking to recover fees is debatable. Figure 14 illustrates how this might work in practice.

Getting Paid

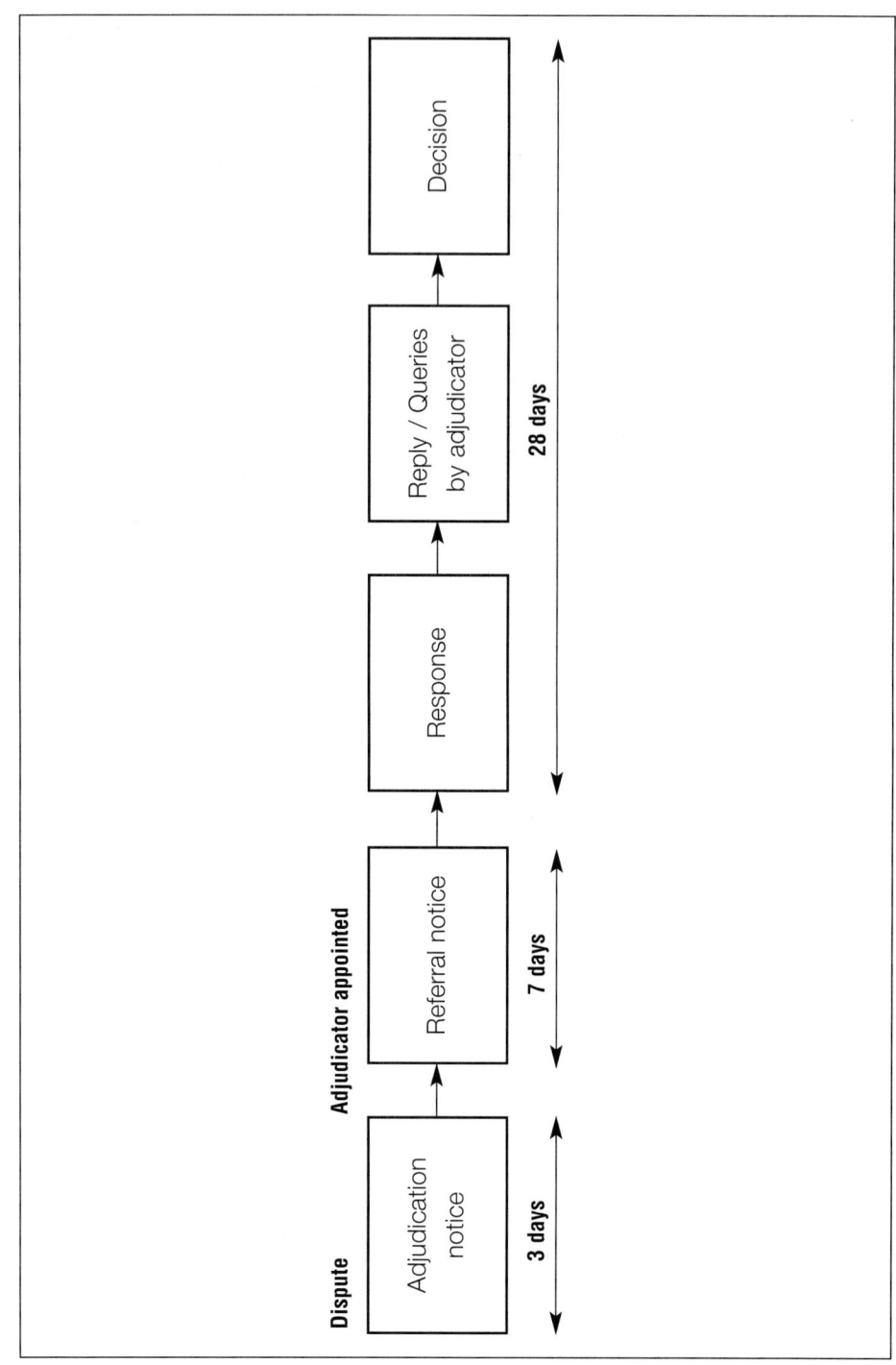

Figure 14: Adjudication of simple fee claim

Adjudication

In short, adjudication provides an attractive option in attempts to recover fees.

The possibility that the parties to a domestic contract might agree to have their differences settled by adjudication has recently been explored in *Picardi* v *Cuniberti*.[8] This case also provides a salutary lesson to architects who fail properly to conclude the terms of their appointment. The importance of this case is such that it is considered in a little detail. The case concerned extensive refurbishment works to a large private house. The claimant was engaged by the owners of the house, the defendants to act as architect in respect of the refurbishment works. It was common ground that he had presented them with a completed copy of CE/99 for signature. There was also common ground that the appointment was not signed, and at trial the defendants referred to previous unhappy experiences with other building works. The architect maintained that he had offered to go through the terms of the document with the defendants. This was contested but, in any event, it was not done. Nonetheless, fee accounts were rendered and in many instances paid. Disputes occurred when certain fee invoices were not paid. The architect maintained:

- that the defendant's conduct in engaging him and paying invoices showed that by conduct they accepted that the terms of CE/99 were incorporated in accordance with the draft he had presented them; and
- that this incorporated the provisions permitting disputes to be referred to adjudications.

His Honour Judge Toulmin QC CMC found as follows:

- If an architect wishes to maintain that the terms of a standard form contract are incorporated into his or her contract with the client, the terms of that contract must be explained to his or her client where that client is a private individual.
- This applies particularly to matters such as the adjudication clause, which affects the rights that the client would otherwise have in respect of disputes.
- If the architect maintains that his or her client has accepted particular terms by virtue of his or her conduct, that conduct needs to be clearly and

unequivocally referable to the terms argued for. Hence it was insufficient simply to send on account invoices since this could not be tied to any particular acceptance of the terms of CE/99. Certainly it could not be referred back to the payment terms within the appointment.

The effect was that the architect could not claim that the contract between himself and his client incorporated the terms of CE/99 and particularly the adjudication clause. Hence the adjudication he had called seeking to recover his fees was a nullity. The lessons that this case provides in relation to the importance of agreeing the terms of appointments are self-evident. It goes without saying that if architects fail to explain to their clients the terms on which they are expecting to act, they do so at their peril. At least where private individuals are concerned, an architect is going to find it difficult, if not impossible, to maintain that contract terms have been incorporated other than by express agreement.

Enforcement

Adjudication decisions are enforceable unless and until revised by subsequent proceedings. Where a decision is made and the opposing party does not pay the sum awarded, the simplest solution is to issue a claim in the Technology and Construction Court. Following one of the earliest enforcement decisions, the practice has grown up of applying for time limits to be abridged such that the matter can be brought before a judge within a matter of days.[9]

The application should be supported by a witness statement which need only recite the fact of the adjudicator's decision and ask for judgement for that sum. The opposing party is entitled to respond and at the hearing, which is generally now of no more than an hour's duration, the court will determine whether the claimant should have judgement there and then or whether there are any matters requiring more detailed investigation. Assuming that the adjudicator's decision has been properly obtained, the court will generally give judgement which can then be enforced.

Adjudication

Endnotes:

1 The exclusion of such contracts from the scope of the Act has never been adequately explained, and the fact that there is no proposal to amend this state of affairs is unsatisfactory.

2 Although it is worth making the suggestion, by this point it is often too late and any suggestion from the architect, however sensible, will often fall on deaf ears.

3 Rule 18.

4 See *Picardi* v *Cuniberti*.

5 The decision in *Discain* v *Opecprime Developments Ltd* [2000] BLR 402 provides a good example.

6 A common problem has been the assertion by one of the parties that there is not in fact a dispute, see *Fast Track* v *Morrison* (2000) 75 Con LR 33.

7 The clumsy terms 'referral notice' and 'adjudication notice' are clearly overdue for reform.

8 Unreported, transcript, 19 December 2002.

9 See *Outwing* v *H Randall and Sons Ltd* [1999] BLR 156.

Getting Paid

9 Legal expenses insurance

Introduction
Legal expenses insurance is insurance cover in respect of the risk of paying legal costs following a claim. Generally it is only available to the party bringing the claim, and in theory can be taken out in respect of the risk of paying the party's own costs and those of the opponent. It takes two main forms, pre-event cover (PEC) and after the event cover (ATE).

Pre-event cover
This closely resembles any other form of cover which is purchased for a particular period. The insured is likely to be asked by the broker for a brief record of their claims history over recent insurance periods and if this is satisfactory will be offered cover in respect of particular types of claims for a period commencing when the offer of insurance is accepted. If during the period of insurance the insured becomes involved in a dispute of the type covered the insured will notify insurers. Depending on the nature of the cover bought, they will be insured in respect of the risk of being obliged to pay their own costs or those of their opponent or both. Generally this type of cover is relatively inexpensive and is reasonably widely available.

After the event cover
Insurance is taken out in respect of a particular claim. The dispute will already have arisen. By contrast with PEC, where the risk is that during the period of insurance a dispute will arise, here the dispute has already arisen and hence the risk is that the claim will fail and the claimant will face not only liability for their own costs but also those of the opponent.

The question for insurers is therefore whether the dispute in question appears to have good prospects of success and hence the extent of the risk, if cover is offered, is that of being faced with a costs order. The insurer will accordingly undertake a reasonably detailed appraisal of the claim and its prospects before making an offer of insurance cover. This form of insurance has only become available in the last few years and is comparatively expensive.

Getting Paid

How it works

Like any other form of insurance, legal expenses insurance is concerned with providing cover against the risk of a particular eventuality occurring. With both types of cover the ultimate risk is that the claim will be unsuccessful and the claimant will face an order that they should pay not only their own costs but those of the opponent.

For most architects' practices considering bringing claims for unpaid fees, legal expenses insurance has an obvious attraction. Where adjudication is not available there will always be the risk that an unsuccessful claim will be followed by an adverse costs order. Since the costs involved in bringing the claim may well exceed the sums in dispute, the decision to bring a claim will always be one which involves a high measure of risk.

Legal expenses cover, at its simplest, will provide cover against the risk of an adverse costs order. However this concept needs to be examined. Different insurance products will provide differing levels of cover and in each instance it should be understood what precisely is being purchased.

- **All costs:** cover is provided against the risk of being ordered to pay the other side's costs and one's own costs. In the case of ATE policies this is uncommon simply because the costs of providing this type of cover tend to be prohibitive.
- **Other side's costs only:** cover is limited to the other party's costs. The insured is faced with paying their own costs in the event that the claim is unsuccessful.
- **Other side's costs and part of own costs:** as above save that the cover extends typically to a proportion of one's own costs, usually involving a percentage of one's own legal costs and disbursements.

In the second and third arrangements described above, the insurance provider will normally stipulate that the architect's legal advisers should enter into a form of conditional fee arrangement (CFA) whereby in the event that the claim is unsuccessful the architect's legal advisers will either forgo their fees or will be limited to recovering the proportion of their fees covered by insurance.

It is worth noting that in almost all cases the policy will also seek to define what is meant by an 'unsuccessful' claim, that is to say a claim which will lead to the policy responding. It follows from Chapter 7 that this will not merely be where the claim fails but will also cover situations where the opposing party has made a 'Calderbank' or CPR Part 36 offer and the claimant fails to beat it such that the claimant is ordered to pay the defendant's costs from a particular point in the proceedings. The majority of policies will provide that if an offer is made above a particular 'threshold' figure the insurer has the right to insist upon it being accepted or reserves the right to withdraw cover.

In most cases the insurance policy will also specifically exclude situations where the claim, though successful, is not paid as a result of the insolvency of the other party. Since most policies will require a measure of investigation to be undertaken as a condition of offering cover this should be limited to cases where the financial standing of the opposing party declines during the progress of the claim.

CFAs, success fees and premiums

Most legal expenses policies will not provide cover in respect of the entirety of the architect's own legal costs. At best, cover will be provided for a proportion of those costs together with disbursements. Of course in the event that the claim is successful, the architect will be entitled to recover the costs from the opposing party but, in the absence of a clear agreement to the contrary, the architect remains primarily liable for their own legal costs. This liability will arise where, for example; the defendant becomes insolvent and fails to meet the architect's costs or where the matter is settled on a 'wrapped up' basis whereby the architect agrees to accept a lump sum expressed to include costs.

Accordingly, most forms of legal expense cover contain a recommendation and sometimes a requirement that the architect's solicitor agrees to conduct the case on the basis of a CFA. At its simplest this is an arrangement whereby the solicitor agrees to take the case on the basis that they will receive no, or at best a greatly reduced, fee in the event that the claim is unsuccessful, but that the solicitor will receive an enhanced fee if the claim succeeds.

Getting Paid

Although the notion of carrying out works on a speculative basis where fees are linked to the outcome of the project is second nature to most architects (and is dealt with in Chapter 4) this type of arrangement has only been part of the legal landscape for the last decade. Prior to this it was asserted by the bodies who regulate the legal profession that to link payment to results was to compromise the independence and professional integrity of the legal profession. Since lawyers owe a duty not only to their client but also to the court, it was felt that this would suffer if the lawyer's right to payment depended upon securing a particular result. However, it has been acknowledged that while this view reflects an ideal world, its effect has been to deprive a great part of the population of the right to seek redress through the courts, simply because they could not afford to do so. Hence the Courts and Legal Services Act 1994 and the Access to Justice Act 1999 have largely removed the prohibition against lawyers conducting matters on a contingency basis.

The relevant provisions of the Access to Justice Act 1999 are summarised as follows:[1]

- section 27 confirms that CFA's are lawful and, provided they are in writing, are enforceable. Success fees are limited to a maximum uplift of 100 per cent;
- section 28 makes lawful litigation funding agreements, i.e., an agreement by one person to fund proceedings brought by another person, again provided that the request is in writing;
- section 29 provides that where a party's costs include the cost of an insurance policy taken out against the risk of incurring a liability for costs in those proceedings, the cost payable to them may include the costs in respect of the policy.

The CFA provides the architect with a very useful method of pursuing bad debts. The risk of having to pay their own lawyers' costs is greatly reduced and the lawyers fund most or all of them throughout the course of the action.
The architect has the encouragement of knowing that, as the lawyers are prepared to gamble their fees on a successful outcome, the case must have merit; and it places them in a much stronger negotiating position with the client.

However, many solicitors are not prepared to take cases on this basis. Those who do will, understandably, take only those cases which have a good chance of success. Therefore the architect's case must be carefully documented and well presented in order that its merits are clear. There must be little risk that an unforeseen matter, e.g. a meeting which was not recorded, will crop up that could destroy the case. After the architect finds a solicitor who is willing to accept an instruction on a CFA basis, he or she will be suitably prepared to negotiate with the client from a position of strength.

A typical CFA is set out in Appendix 5. The crucial provisions are as follows:

- the solicitor agrees that they will either only charge fees in the event that a successful outcome is achieved, or will limit their fees to a specific proportion of the fee otherwise chargeable;
- the client will usually remain liable for certain disbursements which are inappropriate for treatment on a CFA basis (usually experts' fees);
- in the event of a successful outcome, the solicitor will be entitled to recover their full fee, plus in some instances a success fee up to a maximum uplift of 100 per cent of the normal fee;
- the notion of what constitutes success needs to be defined with care: usually this will be defined as recovery above a certain figure or proportion of the claim;
- provision needs to be made for what happens in the event that the sums awarded to the claimant are not paid by reason of the insolvency of the defendant. This is a difficult issue: invariably the parties will be well advised to undertake careful investigation of the opposing party's means before the claim is commenced.

This leads to the question of success fees. Again this is a concept understood by most architects but is relatively new to lawyers. Under the provisions of the 1999 Act, summarised above, the lawyer is entitled to recover a success fee limited to a maximum uplift of 100 per cent of the 'normal' fee and this success fee can be recovered from the opposing party as part of the successful party's fees, subject to the important proviso that such success fees must be reasonable. It is clear from the most recent authority[2] that the courts will take

Getting Paid

each case on its individual merits and that there are no hard and fast rules.[3]

Finally it is also clear from the 1999 Act that, again subject to a test of reasonableness, the premium payable for cover will be recoverable. Again it is likely that the courts will view each case on its individual merits.

Some pros and cons

From the perspective of the architect, the decision to take out PEC insurance will inevitably be one based on balancing cost and risk. In the event that the period of insurance passes without a claim, it might be thought that the expenditure has been wasted. As with any other type of insurance, this is a false analysis: insurance is bought because there is a risk that it will be needed at some stage and if it is that it will more than pay for itself.

That view is confirmed by comparing the cost of PEC with ATE: the former will invariably be a small fraction of the latter. Where the architect takes out ATE insurance, there is no doubt that it will involve him or her in a considerable expense. So what does this actually buy? Of course, in the event that the claim fails, and the architect is ordered to pay the opponent's costs, the architect will be protected from this risk.

On a slightly subtler level, it also sends an important signal to an opponent. It is not unusual for the more confrontational of clients to indicate to the architect that, since the client's resources are greater than those of the architect and the architect will not be able to afford to bring proceedings, the architect will not be able to pursue their claim. The fact that the architect has obtained insurance and therefore has the means to pursue the claim may convey to the client that it cannot necessarily rely on defeating the claim simply by attempting to spin proceedings out until the architect's means are exhausted. However it is important to note that insurers are becoming increasingly aware of the increased bargaining power which the offer of and ATE policy brings, and are increasingly stipulating that the offer cannot be disclosed to the client prior to payment of the permission or preparation of it.

Legal expenses insurance

This will also affect the 'balance of power' in the claim. Chapter 7 looked at applications for security for costs. Quite legitimately, the architect's opponent will consider this at an early stage in the dispute. The nature of the architect's profession is that most practices are relatively modest and those which are limited companies will generally not show large cash surpluses in their accounts. Hence they will ordinarily be vulnerable to applications for security for costs. The existence of legal expenses insurance will generally serve to thwart such applications. Provided the policy remains in force, the opponent's costs position is protected. It may be that the opponent will seek to have the policy 'charged' with their interest – this is unlikely to be objectionable, although in reality it is unnecessary. What this inevitably means is that if for any reason the policy ceases to be in force, the protection will end. It is therefore likely that any application for security will need to be met with an undertaking on the part of the architect to the effect that if the policy lapses, the opponent will be notified and the opponent will obviously at that point be free to resume their application.

Readers of the architectural and construction press will be aware that applications for security have been criticised as no more than a ploy by which legitimate claims are frustrated. The comment which is made in some quarters is that all that the policy of insurance does is to provide a means of side-stepping such applications, without necessarily dealing with the essential point of principle, that is to say the right to bring such applications in the first place. This view is understandable, if misguided. There is nothing inherently unfair about the right to apply for security for costs. The mere fact that one party is of lesser financial means does not necessarily mean there is merit in the claim: sometimes the reverse is true.

Of course, one of the difficulties with ATE cover is its cost. While different products will vary in cost, depending on the nature and extent of cover purchased, a useful yardstick is that the rate on line – the cost of the premium measured as a percentage of the sum insured – will be about 20 to 30 per cent. That is to say that if the sum covered is £15,000, the premium cost will be at least £3,000. This is a considerable sum for many in private practice. Since few insurers will be willing to consider writing cover for lesser sums, partly because the administrative costs of doing so make such an exercise uneconomic, but more importantly because such a sum will often be the minimum level of protection which will be necessary if the case proceeds to a contested hearing, there will be many claims for which this sort of cover is not a practical option.

One option which has been considered in this context is that of finding a lending institution who will advance the cost of the premium to the claimant, securing it by way of a charge on the proceeds of the claim. This approach has its origins in personal injury claims. At present, although this approach has been used on larger claims, it has not been deployed on the sort of smaller disputes with which architect's fee claims are typically concerned. The adverse publicity surrounding the application of these techniques to personal injury litigation means that it may be some time before a way to apply this to small architect's fee recovery claims is found.

An allied concern is whether legal expenses insurance is the answer in all cases. The paradox for claimants and insurers is this: insurers will be looking to provide ATE cover in cases where the prospects of success are high and will not be keen to insure the more speculative cases; on the other hand, if the claim borders upon being a 'dead certainty' (admittedly a rarity in any form of legal proceedings), the claimant might be better advised attempting to negotiate some form of CFA, without resorting to insurance.

It is also important to remember that neither form of cover provides protection against the possibility that the opposing party becomes unable to pay the claim. With PEC claims, the claimant is strongly recommended to research carefully the financial standing of the opponent before a claim is commenced. With ATE claims, it is likely that if insurers feel that the standing of the opponent is questionable, they will decline to offer cover. In either case, insurers do not offer cover against the risk of the opponent's insolvency, and an entirely separate species of insurance known as deficiency of damages cover exists to deal with this.

It is also worth noting that, at the moment, legal expenses cover will generally not be available for adjudication. This is partly because the speed at which adjudications are commenced and dealt with generally means that it is impractical to set up cover, but more significantly because most forms of cover provide insurance against the risk of an adverse costs order, which will not be a consideration in most adjudications.

The final point which needs to be understood is that of the relationship between claims made under legal expenses cover and professional indemnity cover. Where the claim for fees is met by a counterclaim alleging professional negligence, it is of paramount importance to ensure that professional indemnity insurers are kept regularly and accurately informed of the progress of the claim. If it transpires that in fact the prospects for the fee claim are less good than was anticipated at the outset, it is crucial that professional indemnity insurers are able to make an informed judgement whether to take over the conduct of the matter, which henceforward will take the form of defending a claim for negligence as opposed to pursuing a claim for fees.

Endnotes:

1 A full version is available at www.hmso.gov.uk

2 See *Callery* v *Gray* [2002] 3 All ER 417: given an opportunity to provide some guidance of general application, the courts declined to do so.

3 In particular it will be noted that all of the cases to date have dealt with personal injury claims and particularly matters conducted by claims handling agencies.

Getting Paid

Appendix 1: Case Study 1 materials

Letter 1

Jim Slip RIBA
1, The Avenue
Springfield

May 1

Ned Clump
Ned Clump Industrial Limited
The Industrial Estate
Springfield

Dear Ned

The Big House, Park Lane

Following our meeting I am writing to set out some proposals. First, we agreed that the Big House will be refurbished, part will be used as office premises, part as your new London residence. We also agreed that I would develop my initial sketches into a detailed design to be submitted for planning purposes. We have agreed that you would use Liddle & Nudge Limited as builders and that a standard form contract would be used. For my part I suggest that my fees are calculated on the basis of 11 per cent of the eventual build cost. We could cap this if you would prefer.

I look forward to hearing from you.

Yours sincerely

Getting Paid

Letter 2

Ned Clump
Ned Clump Offshore Limited
P.O. BOX 123
Tortola

May 10

Jim Slip
1, The Avenue
Springfield

Dear Jim

The Big House, Park Lane

Thank you for your letter of 1 May. I agree that we need to finalise various items and look forward to hearing from you in relation to the detailed design because I am keen that this matter should progress with all speed. In particular we need to get on with determining the scope and exact cost of the works. I am not sure that I have yet finalised exactly what I want, although it is imperative that we start work as soon as possible.

As for fees, we need to achieve agreement for this. I would prefer a lump sum.

Yours sincerely

Minutes of meeting (extract)

> 1.04 Terms of Appointment discussed. JS will send NC copy of CE/99.
>
> Revision B drawing circulated. Alternative columns to make use of light will be considered. JS will consider whether alternative design needed.

Minutes of pre-start meeting (extract)

> 1.04.1 Terms of CE/99 discussed. JS and NC to meet in order to settle terms review. JS to write to NC re frequency of inspections and site visits.

Appendix 2: Checklist

1. Client
- Precise identity of client, individual or company
- Financial status of client
- Form when the instructions taken

2. Terms
- What am I required to do?
- What if extra work is required?
- How will this be instructed?
- By whom?

3. Forms of appointment
- How is appointment to be documented?
- Standard form or bespoke contract?
- Has this been approved by professional indemnity insurers?
- Warranties?
  To whom are they to be given?
  Have they been approved by insurers?

4. Fees
- How calculated?
- When are they to be paid?
- Payments for extra work
- Interest on the payment
- Suspension for non-payment

Appendix 3: Glossary of terms

Acknowledgement of service: The form lodged with the court indicating whether the defendant intends to contest the claim.

Allocation questionnaire (AQ): Form filled in by the parties indicating brief details of the dispute to enable the court to determine the most effective way of dealing with the matter.

Case management conference (CMC): Hearing used on larger cases where the court gives directions for timetabling the case.

Claim form: The document by which proceedings are formally commenced.

Disclosure of documents: Procedure where the parties make available to each other the documents on which each intends to rely.

Fast track: The court's procedure for dealing with cases where over £5,000 but under £15,000 is at stake.

Multi-track: The court's procedure for dealing with larger claims.

Particulars of claim: The document setting out the details of the claim.

Preliminary issues: Procedures whereby certain questions are determined by the court which are intended to avoid the need for full trial.

Small claims track: The court's procedure for dealing with cases where under £5,000 is at stake.

Statement of case: A formal document (such as particulars of claim) in which a party sets out the facts and contentions they intend to rely upon.

Summary judgement: Procedure where matters are dealt with without full trial.

Technology and Construction Court: The division of the High Court where construction and engineering (and related) disputes are heard.

Appendix 4: Claim form and particulars of claim

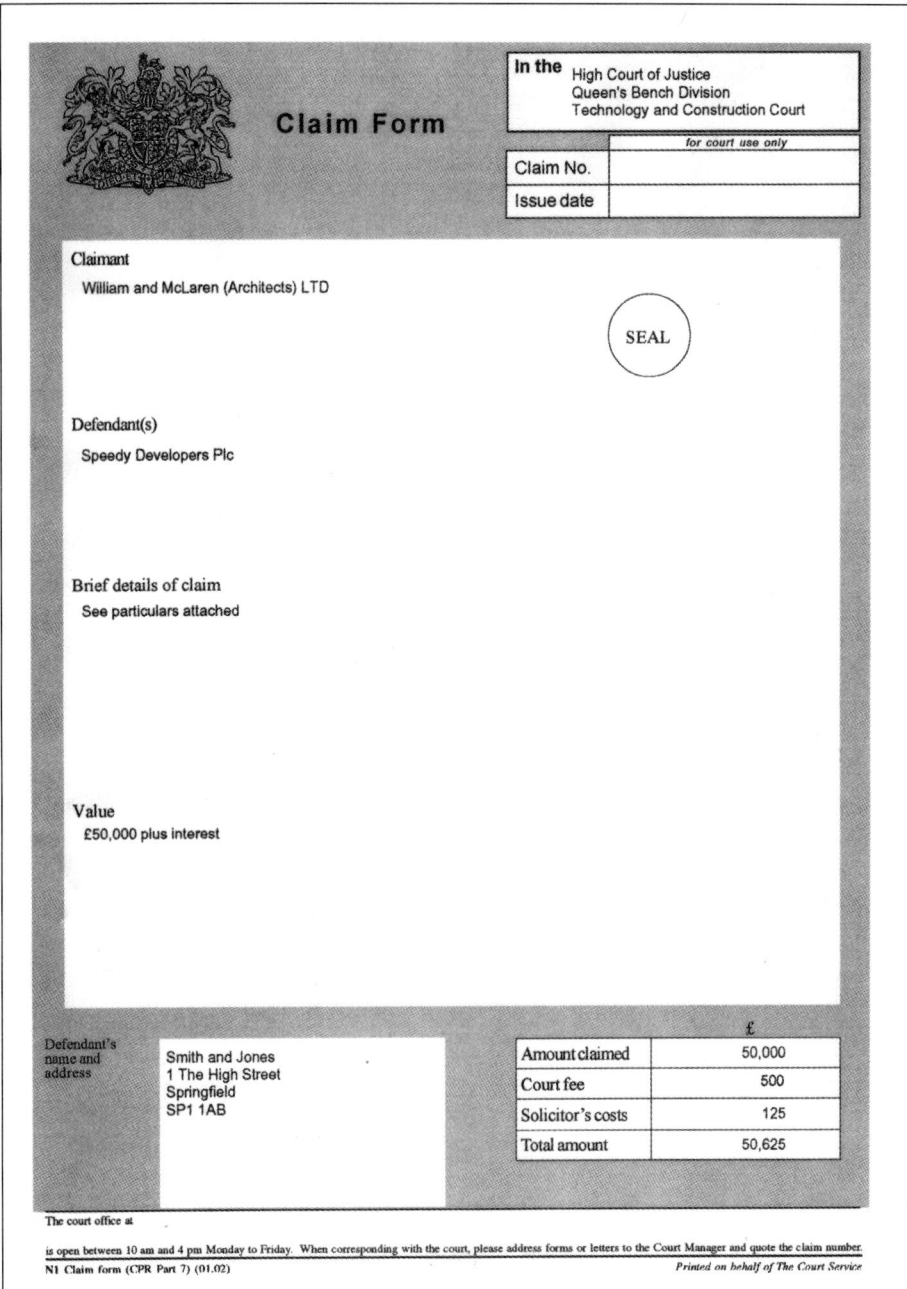

Claim form and particulars of claim

Claim No.	

Does, or will, your claim include any issues under the Human Rights Act 1998? ☐ Yes ☑ No

Particulars of Claim (attached)~~(to follow)~~

Statement of Truth
* ~~(I believe)~~(The Claimant believes) that the facts stated in these particulars of claim are true.
* I am duly authorised by the claimant to sign this statement

Full name _John Smith_

Name of claimant's solicitor's firm _Smith and Jones_

signed _J Smith_ position or office held _Partner_

*(Claimant)(Litigation friend)(Claimant's solicitor) (if signing on behalf of firm or company)

*delete as appropriate

Smith and Jones
1 The High Street
Springfield
SP1 1AB

Claimant's or claimant's solicitor's address to which documents or payments should be sent if different from overleaf including (if appropriate) details of DX, fax or e-mail.

This document is available at www.lcd.gov.uk/civil/prorules_fin/menus/forms.htm

Getting Paid

Claim Form

IN THE HIGH COURT OF JUSTICE   CASE NO
QUEENS BENCH DIVISION
TECHNOLOGY AND CONSTRUCTION COURT

BETWEEN

Williams and Maclaren (Architects) Limited   Claimants

-and-

Speedy Developers Plc   Defendants

Particulars of Claim

1. The Claimants are architects. The Defendants are property developers.

2. By a contract in writing, the Claimants agreed to act as architects on behalf of the Defendants in relation to a project, which the Defendants were undertaking, known as The Big House, Park Lane, London, W1 ('the Appointment').

3. The Appointment was in writing and dated 1 January 2002 and was in the form of Architect's Appointment, standard form SFA/99, executed under seal. A copy is at Schedule 1.

4. The Claimants will refer to the whole of the Appointment but the important terms are as follows:
Clause 2.1: Architect's obligations to perform the services in accordance with duty of care.
Clause 2.2: Architect to perform services without an appointment.

Clause 5.1: Fees to be calculated in accordance with Third Schedule.
Clause 5.10: Final date for payment to be 30 days from date of rendering account.
Clause 5.11: Excludes right of set-off.
Clause 5.13: Interest on late payment.

5. The Claimants performed their functions as architects in accordance with the terms of the Appointment.

6. The Claimants made applications for payment as follows:

    | 1 March 2002: | £5,000 |
    | 1 June 2002: | £20,000 |
    | 1 September 2002: | £35,000 |
    | | £60,000 |

    each of which was in the form of an invoice, a copy of which is at Schedule 2. Payment of each was due 28 days after the invoice was discussed.

7. The Defendants have to date paid only the sum of £10,000 as a result of which the sum of £50,000 remains due and owing.

8. The Claimants have requested payment. The Defendants have failed or refused to make the payment.

9. The Claimants are entitled to interest on all sums due.
    And the Claimants claim:
    (i)   £50,000
    (ii) Interest

Appendix 5: Conditional fee agreement

your reference
our reference   date

CONDITIONAL FEE AGREEMENT

Date of Agreement ... 2003

We [name of solicitor]

And

You [name of client]

AGREE AS FOLLOWS:

1. **This Conditional Fee Agreement ('CFA')** forms the basis on which we will accept instructions to act for you in your claim against ... ('your Opponent') for damages or other monetary sums arising from or in connection with the circumstances described below.

    Brief Particulars of Claim:
    Claim against:

    until the case is won or lost or this Agreement is terminated.

    This CFA does not cover any counterclaim against you or your Insured.

2. **This CFA** sets out how costs incurred by us in advising you and in acting for you in arbitration proceedings or proceedings in a court of first instance (county court or High Court) in England and Wales, excluding the costs of any counterclaim, will be dealt with.

Conditional fee agreement

3.1 **If you win** the case, you will pay our disbursements, our basic charges and our success fee (see below for details). If proceedings have to be commenced, you will normally be entitled to recover all or part of our disbursements and of our basic charges, including Counsel's basic fees, and of our success fee from your Opponent. If the claim is settled before proceedings are commenced, you may be unable to recover costs from your Opponent.

3.2 **If you lose** the case, you will pay our disbursements, including Counsel's basic fees unless he has entered into a CFA with us, and you will almost certainly also be liable to pay your Opponent's costs and disbursements.

3.3 **If you terminate** this CFA before the case is won or lost, you will forthwith pay our disbursements, including Counsel's basic fees, and our basic charges to date of termination. If you subsequently go on to win the case, you will also pay our success fee and, if Counsel has entered into a CFA with us, Counsel's success fee, in which instance the percentages in paragraph 6 below will only be applied to our basic charges and Counsel's basic fees to the date on which you terminated this CFA.

4.1 **'Win'**
You will be deemed to 'win' when the case is decided in your favour against your Opponent or against one of several Opponents by agreement, or an arbitration award, or an order or judgment of the Court. If you win by reason of an arbitration award or order or judgment of the Court, and your Opponent appeals, paragraph 11 below will apply.

4.2 **'Lose'**
You will be deemed to 'lose' the case when an arbitrator or a Court has dismissed all proceedings or you have discontinued them on our advice or with our agreement.

Getting Paid

5. **Basic charges**

5.1 We will appoint the following persons to work on this case at the hourly charging rates shown:

Name	Status	Rate
	Partner	
	Senior Solicitor	
	Assistant Solicitor	
	Legal Executive	
	Legal Assistant	
	Paralegal	
	Trainee Solicitor	

5.2 We reserve the right to change the composition of the above team if we consider this necessary or appropriate but only after consulting you. These hourly rates are our rates for the above persons concerned working on this case and reflect what we reasonably expect to recover on an assessment of costs. The rates are in line with Appendix 2: Guideline Figures for the Summary Assessment of Costs as issued by the Court Service. Our rates will be subject to review in April/May of each year. We will not increase our rates without prior consultation. Our 'basic charges' are our fees based on the number of hours worked by the above persons at the hourly rates shown.

6. **Success Fee**

6.1 The success fee will be …% of our basic charges and, if Counsel has entered into a CFA with us, …% of Counsel's basic fees. This percentage reflects our and, if Counsel has entered into a CFA with us, Counsel's estimation of the difficulty of the case and of the level of risk we are taking. Our reasons for calculating the success fee at

Conditional fee agreement

this level are set out in Schedule 1 below. The maximum success fee permitted under current legislation is 100% of our basic charges and, if applicable, 100% of Counsel's basic fees.

6.2   You cannot recover from your Opponent that part of the success fee which relates to the cost to us of financing the delay in our receiving our costs. We estimate that part of the success fee at 7% per annum, but this percentage may be increased or reduced by the Arbitrator or Court on any assessment of costs. This figure represents the cost of financing the case over the course of one year, which is the likely timescale up to the conclusion of the claim.

6.3   If you win the case, we may be obliged to disclose to the Arbitrator or Court and to your Opponent the reasons for setting the success fee at the level shown above.

6.4   If in assessing our costs the Arbitrator or Court disallows any part of the success fee on the grounds that it is unreasonably high in view of what we knew or the Arbitrator or Court considers we should have known at the time when it was agreed, you will not have to pay us the amount disallowed.

6.5   If we agree with your Opponent that they should pay a success fee at a lower percentage than that set out in this agreement, the amount of our success fee will be reduced accordingly and you will not have to pay us the amount by which the success fee has been thus reduced.

6.6   If your Opponent makes an offer in settlement which includes payment of our basic charges and a success fee at a lower percentage than that set out in this agreement, you will not instruct us to accept that offer unless we are willing to accept that reduced percentage.

Getting Paid

7. **Counsel's Fees**

   We expect that Counsel will in most cases be instructed to act under separate CFAs between them and us. We will discuss with you the terms of any such agreement and in particular the proposed success fee (which will generally be set at the same level as ours) at the appropriate time. If Counsel is not acting under a CFA, his or her fees will be treated as a disbursement and will be payable by you as set out below.

8. **Disbursements**

   You will pay our disbursements including Court fees, expert fees and Counsel's basic fees (unless he has entered into a CFA with us) as the case proceeds. We will send you disbursement invoices in the normal way. Counsel's 'basic fees' are the fees which Counsel would be entitled to charge if he/she had not entered into a CFA with us.

9. **Interlocutory Costs**

   In CFA cases Judges are required to 'give consideration' to staying orders for costs of interim hearings until the conclusion of the proceedings. If, however, your Opponent obtains an order for an immediate payment of his or her interim costs, these will be payable by you at the time.

10. **Offers and Payments into Court**

10.1 **If your Opponent makes a Part 36 or other offer or a payment into Court, we and Counsel will advise you whether you should accept this.**

10.2 If we advise you to accept the Part 36 or other offer or payment into court, but against our advice you wish to continue the proceedings, we (and Counsel if he has entered into a CFA with us) will decide whether we are willing to continue on the existing CFA basis. If either we or Counsel are not so willing, we will only continue to act for you on the basis that:

(a) you will forthwith pay our disbursements, including Counsel's basic fees, and our basic charges up to the date of the Part 36 or other offer or payment into Court, and

(b) from the date of the Part 36 or other offer or payment into Court you will pay our disbursements, including Counsel's basic fees, and our basic charges at 3 monthly intervals or as otherwise agreed. We reserve the right to require payment in advance on account of disbursements and basic charges

(c) if thereafter you accept any offer or payment into Court, or are awarded damages and interest at trial, in an amount which is less than 115 per cent of any previously rejected offer or payment into Court (ignoring for the purpose of this calculation interest for any period between the date of any previously rejected offer or payment into Court and the date of the offer or payment into Court which you do accept or the date of any award in your favour), you will also pay our success fee and, if we have entered into a CFA with Counsel, Counsel's success fee.

10.3 If you reject a Part 36 or other offer or payment into court and accept our advice to continue the proceedings and if you subsequently recover damages in a lesser amount than the offer or payment in, you will only pay our disbursements, including Counsel's basic fees (whether or not we have entered into a CFA with Counsel), and our basic charges incurred prior to the date on which we received notice of the payment into Court. You will not pay a success fee either to us or to Counsel.

Getting Paid

11. **Interest**

    Any interest awarded or otherwise accruing on damages or in relation to disbursements which you have already paid to us will be payable to you. Any interest awarded or otherwise accruing in respect of our disbursements, our basic costs, our success fee or Counsel's success fee will be payable to and retained by us.

12. **Appeals**

    12.1 **If you win** the case by reason of an Arbitrator's award, a Court order or judgment, and your Opponent appeals, you will forthwith pay our disbursements and 75 per cent of our basic charges to date regardless of the final outcome. If you go on to win on appeal, you will pay our success fee and the remaining 25 per cent of our basic charges plus our success fee and, if applicable, Counsel's success fee relating to the trial at first instance and you will also pay our disbursements, our basic charges plus our success fee and, if applicable, Counsel's success fee of the appeal. You will normally be entitled to recover all or part of our disbursements, basic charges and success fee from your Opponent.

    12.2 Conversely, if you go on to lose on appeal, you will not pay the remaining 25 per cent of our basic charges at first instance or any success fee. You will only pay our disbursements relating to the appeal, including Counsel's fees unless he has entered into a CFA with us.

    12.3 **If you lose** the case by reason of an Arbitrator's award, a Court order or judgment, and you accept our advice to appeal, you will pay Counsel's fees (unless he has entered into a CFA with us) and any other disbursements relating to the appeal, i.e. as at first instance. If you go on to win on appeal, you will also pay our basic charges, our success fee and, if he has entered into a CFA with us, Counsel's success fee in respect of the proceedings both at first instance and

Conditional fee agreement

on appeal. You will normally be entitled to recover all or part of our disbursements, basic charges and success fee from your Opponent.

12.4 **If you lose** the case by reason of an Arbitrator's award, a Court order or judgment, and contrary to our advice you decide to appeal, we and Counsel (if he has entered into a CFA with us) will only continue to act for you on the basis that you will pay our disbursements, including Counsel's basic fees, and our basic charges, relating to the appeal, regardless of the final outcome. If you go on to win on appeal, you will pay our disbursements and our basic charges plus our success fee and, if he has entered into a CFA with us, Counsel's success fee, relating to the proceedings at first instance but you will not pay a success fee to us or to Counsel relating to the appeal. You will normally be entitled to recover all or part of these costs from your Opponent.

13. **Explanation of Funding Arrangements**

    Immediately before you signed this CFA we reviewed it with you and verbally explained to you its effect and in particular the following:

    (a) the circumstances in which you will or may be liable to pay our costs and disbursements

    (b) the circumstances in which we may be able to recover our costs and disbursements from your Opponent

    (c) the circumstances in which you may seek an assessment of our charges and disbursements and the procedure for doing so

    (d) whether your potential liability for any costs in this case is insured under any existing contract of insurance

    (e) other methods of financing those costs including funding from your own resources, Community Legal Service Funding, legal expenses insurance and trade union funding

Getting Paid

    (f)   in view of your experience of business and litigation we do not consider that it is appropriate for us to recommend any particular method of financing your liabilities. However, if you require some form of litigation costs insurance to cover your liability for your Opponent's costs (and, as a further option, for our disbursements) if we lose, we shall endeavour to arrange this if you so wish on the understanding that we are not insurance brokers and are not qualified to advise on all products that may be available. If you effect such insurance, you will normally be entitled to recover all or part of the premium from your Opponent provided that we record in this CFA our and/or your reasons for choosing the particular policy. If applicable, these reasons are set out in Schedule 2 below. You have already confirmed to us that you will, in effect, self-insure for this risk rather than pay a premium to a competitor.

(Note: If you win but recover damages and interest of a lesser amount than your Opponent has offered or paid into Court and you are ordered to pay your Opponent's costs from the date of offer or payment into Court, many litigation costs insurance policies provide that any damages and interest recovered shall be applied in payment of your Opponent's costs before it will respond and pay any balance remaining. Also note that litigation costs insurers may have different definitions of 'win' and 'lose' from those in this CFA.)

14. Reporting

14.1   We will report to you at intervals to be agreed (normally at least every four months) and also if your Opponent makes an offer or a payment into Court. We will include in our report any material change in our estimation of the prospects of success and/or any reserve for your Opponent's costs insofar as these are not covered by litigation costs insurance and for our disbursements insofar as these are not covered by a CFA between us and Counsel.

14.2 Any complaints or queries which you may have relating to the subject matter or our conduct of the proceedings or the costs payable under this CFA or otherwise should be addressed in the first instance to the Partner named in paragraph 4 above. If these are not then resolved to your satisfaction, you are invited to contact our Senior Partner.

15. **Disclosure**

We will only disclose the existence of this CFA or, if applicable, the existence of any litigation costs insurance to your Opponent or to any other party if we are obliged to do so by any order or rule of Court or if we consider that it will be in your best interests to do so (e.g. in interim proceedings – see paragraph 9 above).

SCHEDULE 1
The Success Fee

The success fee is set at …% of our basic costs to reflect the following factors:

(a) the fact that if you win we will not be paid our basic costs until the claim is settled or the proceedings come to an end;

(b) our arrangements with you concerning payment of disbursements;

(c) the fact that if you lose, we will not receive any costs;

(d) our assessment of the risks of your case, namely:

Getting Paid

- the usual risks inherent in any proceedings, for example, that witnesses may not come up to proof or that the Tribunal makes incorrect findings of fact or law
- the value of the claim
- adverse evidence from experts as to ...
- there is likely to be a dispute under the Limitation Act 1980
- the case involves an area of law with little/no case law
- a finding by the Tribunal that standard terms apply to the contract and that any liabilities are effectively excluded or restricted
- failure to produce the degree of proof required by the Tribunal to establish some or all of the loss claimed due to unavailable or incomplete records or witness evidence, for example
- liability has been denied by the defendant

The matters set out at paragraphs (a) and (b) above together make up 7 per cent of the increase on basic charges on the basis that the likely timescale up to the conclusion of the claim is one year. The matters at paragraphs (c) and (d) above make up ...% of the increase on basic charges. So the total success fee is ...% as stated above.

SCHEDULE 2
[Where client requires after-the-event insurance]
Litigation Costs Insurance

If, after considering all the circumstances and risks and in the light of the information currently available to us, you and we agree that a litigation costs insurance policy should be effected, we believe that a policy with ... is appropriate to cover your Opponent's charges and disbursements in case you lose, for the following reasons:

- level of indemnity
- deferred payment of premium
- premium waived in the event of defeat
- reputable underwriters/insurance company

Conditional fee agreement

- covers all disbursements including pre-insurance policy
- delegated authority
- level of premium likely to be recoverable
- no interest charged on premium
- it covers the other party's costs on the claimant's failure to beat a defendant's Part 36 offer/payment
- no restriction upon acting under a Conditional Fee Agreement and charging a success fee
- rebate for early settlement

We are not insurance brokers and cannot give advice on all products available.

We confirm that we have no financial interest in recommending this particular insurance agreement.

SIGNED on behalf of [solicitors]
by.....................................
Partner

SIGNED on behalf of [client]
by..

Index

Access to Justice Act 1999
108, 126
Acknowledgement of service
87, 93, 94,137
Adjudication
32, 64, 66, 109–20
ARB Standards of Conduct
19
Arbitration Act 1996
9, 68, 78, 79, 85, 101, 105, 106
Arbitration procedure
101
Architect's guide to fee negotiation
35
Architect's Job Book
21, 37
Calderbank offers
98, 125
CE/95
11, 12, 32, 67
Civil Procedure Rules
78, 86, 93, 97, 98, 99, 101, 106, 108
Claim form
85, 86, 87, 137, 138
Conditional Fee Agreement
9, 72, 142
Costs
32, 33, 67, 68, 89, 105–107, 111
Courts and Legal Services Act 1994
126
Disclosure
74, 75, 84, 90, 97–8, 137, 151
Expert evidence
84, 88, 90, 92, 91, 92–3

Fast track
69, 88, 89–91, 137
Housing Grants, Construction and Regeneration Act (HGCRA) 1996
9, 18–9, 32, 53, 61, 66, 109, 112
Human Rights Act 1998
41
Late Payment of Commercial Debts (Interest) Act 1998
17, 19, 32
Legal expense insurance
9, 97, 123–31, 149–53
Litigation
68, 71, 85–101
Mediation
64, 67–8
Multi-track
88, 90, 91, 97, 102, 137
Part 36 offers and payments into court
97, 98–100, 125, 146, 147, 153
Particulars of claim
86–7, 137, 138–41
Pre-action Protocols for the Construction and Engineering Disputes
88, 90, 102
Requirement of reasonableness
24, 40, 53, 61, 128
RIBA Plan of Work
21, 37
Right of architect to suspend work for non-payment
31, 62, 63
Right to payment
17–30
Scheme for Construction Contracts
18, 113, 155
Security for costs
32, 72, 77, 95–7, 129

Set-off
49–55
SFA/92
31, 32
SFA/99
21, 22, 32, 34, 36, 39, 45, 51, 55, 62, 63, 67, 72, 76, 77, 87, 89, 96, 105, 107, 109, 111, 140
Summary judgement
88, 93–5, 137
SW/96
32
Terms of engagement and fees
35
Unfair Contract Terms Act 1977
19, 53
Woolf Reforms
9, 69, 77, 97, 105, 106